FOURSQUARE BOOKS

OLD DAME DANCING

OLD DAME DANCING

Essays From The Eighth Decade

Nancy Parsons

OLD DAME DANCING
Nancy Parsons

Published by
The Cheshire Press
A Division of The Cheshire Group, Inc.
PO Box 2090
Andover, MA 01810
www.cheshirepress.com

All rights reserved. No part of this book may be
reproduced or transmitted in any form or by any means
without the express written consent of the author, except for
the inclusion of quotations in reviews.

Copyright © 2016 by Nancy Parsons

ISBN: 978-0-9960210-7-4
Library of Congress Control Number: 2016941377

Printed in the United States of America

 Any resemblance to individuals or occupations is purely coincidental.
All trademarks used herein are for identification only and are used
without intent to infringe on theowner's trademarks or other
property rights.

Parsons, Nancy
OLD DAME DANCING

Drawings by Don Doyle

OLD DAME DANCING

For the Girls of '42
Karen, Joyce, Sally, Linda, Jan, Lyn and Sue
beautiful old dames, every one

and especially to the memory of
Katie

OLD DAME DANCING

Also by Nancy Parsons

More From The Better Mousetrap
with Dick Amsterdam

Bald As A Bean: The Experience of Sudden Hair Loss

Abigail's Unicorn

Ye Canna Join In Oor Games
Memories of a Scottish-American Childhood

Brothers of War: The P.O.W. Experience
with James F. Arsenault

The Dog That Managed Hedge Funds

∼ The Nell Bane Novels ∼
Two-Thirds of a Ghost
The Ghost Works A Puzzle
The Ghost Ties A Double Knot
The Ghost Paints A Portrait
The Ghost Lays The Ghosts To Rest

OLD DAME DANCING

"You're standing in the middle of a roomful of people," Grace said, "and suddenly you realize you're the oldest person there. It's odd, because you reach this level without any experience, and you're expected to know your role. And you expect, expected, yourself to be wise as well, and it comes as a great letdown to know you're just the same person, but older. So you go by the old standbys, advise moderation one day and vision the next, because some days you're satisfied and happy and some days you feel there are too few days left to seize. You have to take old age personally."

Beachcombing for a Shipwrecked God
Joe Coomer

OLD DAME DANCING

CONTENTS

THIS TIME OF ABATEMENT   13

MY BODY HAS AN AGE, I DON'T
   I Don't Seem Old To Me   17
   Aging Friends   19
   Looking Up John Candy's Nose   22
   Congenital Drool   24
   Standing on One Leg   27
   An Old Dear   29
   Old Feet   30
   Mother's Day: An Incident   32
   Reminder To Myself   33

IMPERFECT HARMONY
   Marriage and Divine Intervention   37
   A Marriage—2014   40
   Married Young   44
   Memories of a Martini Man   42
   Deciduating   49
   The Bathroom Mirror   52
   The Great Celestial Lost and Found   53
   What If I Were A Witness?   56
   When A Husband Retires   58

ANSWERS TO QUESTIONS NOBODY ASKED
- Why Hepburn Wore Turtlenecks   63
- Why I Hate To Travel   66
- Why We're Still Here   70
- Why I'm Ailurophic   73
- Why We Dine On The Floor   76

OLD DAME WRITING
- Old Dame Writing   81
- Ghostwriters in the Sky   84
- I'll Miss Nell Bane   86
- Irish Thunder   89
- Grace Durrin of Troup Street   91
- Transformations   95
- Move Over, Mr. Webster   98
- An Evening with Joan Parker   101
- Everything Is Memoir   105

LOOKING BACKWARD
- Jumping Rope   111
- The Taste Of Paste   114
- The Way We Wore   117
- The Sounds Of Service   121
- Maggies Sews A Dress   124
- The Best Of It   128

LOOKING FORWARD
- Anticipating The Tipping Points   133
- Our Options Have Changed   137
- And Nobody Limped   140
- Sorry I Missed The Skateboard   142
- Attitude Is Everything   145
- Growing Into Old Age   147

PRESENT PERFECT

An Elderly Pleasure	151
Concessions at Christmas	154
Life Raft	157
A Long Way From The Center Mayfield	161
Those Who Knew Me When	165
One Off The Bucket List	167
Oh, Yes, I Slept Through That One	170
Party	172

SCOOP DISH

Scoop Dish	177
Breaking a Record	178
Social Media For The Anti-Social	181
Charlie Card Bliss	185
Old Dame Kvetching	188
Ending the Christmas Potlatch	191
The Angel Who Stops For A Beer	194
The Motel Clerk	196
The Odyssey of the Purple Hat	197
Things I Will Never Know	199
Things I Think I Do Know	201
This Is Someone's Lunch	202
The Sex Life Of Hangers	204
You Can't Miss It	206
Those Who Rescue Our Hearts	208
There's A Dance In The Old Dame Yet	212

OLD DAME DANCING

When you come to this time of abatement,
To this passage from Summer to Fall,
It is manners to issue a statement
About what you got out of it all.

The Little Old Lady In Lavender Silk
Dorothy Parker

THIS TIME OF ABATEMENT

Eight decades! Oh, that can't be right. But I've counted the decades on my fingers three times and yup, it's come out to eight each time. A friend tried to argue me out of the claim I'd staked. Said it couldn't be eight. Had to be seven. But this is how I figure: birth to age 10 is Decade One. Ages 11 to 20 = Decade Two, 20 to 30 is Three and so on. By the time you're in your seventies, you're deep in the dingles of Decade Eight. So now that I'm here, I guess I, too, will be losing my bloom one of these days, and that means it's time to issue my statement. A number of them, in fact. So here's a collection of expository statements that amount to what I've "got out of it all".

Old Dame Dancing started out as a blog. I had no interest in writing a blog, but Dickie wanted to get a toehold in the blogosphere, so he tried to convince me to write one which he could tinker with and put up online and then presto! we (The Cheshire Group) would would be rubbing virtual shoulders with bloggers and being terribly *au currant*. (Well, this was years ago, before blogs became more common than gum on a sidewalk.) By the time blogs *did* become as common as gum on a sidewalk, Dickie had lost interest in blogging and started fixating on Google AdWords. *Old Dame Dancing* was left languishing in the ether—she with one foot kicking up and her beads flapping. I got to feeling bad about that eventually. Something felt unfinished. So I picked her up, dusted her off and set her dancing again. Most of the blog posts I'd written weren't worthy of redemption, but a few were okay and these made their way into this book. And then, there were a few things I wanted to say about what I got out of my first eight decades, and I wanted to speculate on where I might be going.

So far I've quoted Dorothy Parker, Don Marquis, Joe Coomer and Whoopi Goldberg and we're only two pages into this thing. Well, get used to it. I've been collecting and memorizing quotations and scattering them around during all eight of my decades, and I intend to go right on doing it until dementia turns off my memory machine. Therefore I've salted quotes all through this book like ... well, salt. One of the benefits of age is you can say what you damn well please (well almost what you damn well please). You can be as salty as you want and get away with most of it. So now, with a nod to Marquis's alley cat Mehitabel, I'm going to say it. "Wotthehell, wothehell."

*The older I get,
the better I used to be.*
Unknown

MY BODY HAS AN AGE, I DON'T

OLD DAME DANCING

OLD DAME DANCING

I DON'T SEEM OLD TO ME

Age is a relative thing, I suppose, but here, in the middle of my eighth decade, I don't feel old. To a high school sophomore, I must seem ancient. After all, I was around when Neil Armstrong walked on the moon, when John Kennedy was shot in Dallas, when Dwight Eisenhower was driven down Pennsylvania Avenue to be inaugurated. I was old enough to read the headlines during the Korean War, old enough to play with rationing coins during World War Two, old enough to name most of the players on the Cleveland Indians' roster when they won the pennant in 1948. If you say "phone", I picture a black Bakelite object with a rotary dial. Ask the hourly rate for baby-sitting, and I'd answer thirty-five cents. Suggest "let's go shopping" and I think I'll need my white gloves and a hat.

Memory makes me an emotional fossil, but in my own defense I offer this: I'm also able also operate in a parallel universe. Bakelite phone image notwithstanding, I use Apple Pay on my iphone, subscribe to Netflix and can deal with a global positioning system. I could even text if I wanted to. Only I don't want to.

When I squat, my knees sound like branches breaking in an autumn woods. But! I can still squat. I can still rotate my head 90 degrees on my neck when I back my car out of the driveway. And I can still *remember* the Indians' 1948 lineup, indicating that dementia hasn't completely hijacked my brain.

When she was ninety-six, my Scottish grandmother remarked that inside she was still a girl of seventeen; it was just the girl in the mirror who shocked her. I was jolted when I heard this, and I've thought ever since that there must be something—*something* in us that doesn't age. What is that something? An inordinately healthy self-image? Is it Spirit perhaps? Or just dumb denial? But whatever it is, this *something* sits at the very navel of who we are. And so, like my grandmother, I don't seem old to me.

You, of course, are entitled to your own opinion.

∼

> *Helen Gurley Brown ... died on Monday in Manhattan. She was 90, although parts of her were considerably younger.*
>
> *Margalit Fox:*
> *Obituary of Helen Gurley Brown*

AGING FRIENDS

Dickie has started wearing those clunky white sneakers that fasten with Velcro straps. These, in my opinion, are the hallmark footwear of the aging. They are what you wear when you can no longer bend over comfortably to tie your shoes. They are the first things you see at rest stops when the parade of senior citizens starts descending from the bus. I distinctly remember when Dickie was a disciple of Dress for Success, and now it's Velcro straps. Lo, how the mighty are fallen. It's depressing.

"Dickie!" I want to say. "Shape up! Take those things off and get into your wingtips. Stop broadcasting that you're past seventy-five."

But Dickie isn't my only aging friend. More and more friends have unobtrusive wires running out of their ears, reminding me that my own hearing isn't as acute as it should be. People a decade behind me are having cataracts removed. Perhaps I also have cataracts and I just haven't foud out yet.

And cataracts are minor compared to the other bits of work my aging friends are having done. Original knees are being replaced with clever hinges made of stainless steel. Same goes for hips. I listen in awe to the anatomical name-dropping as my friends speak learnedly of posterior-stabilized knees and cruciate-retaining designs and unicompartmental implants; and they speak with the enthusiasm they once reserved for the newest car models to hit the market each year. The Silent Generation is turning into the Bionic Generation, and half the people I know can't get through an airport metal detector on the first pass.

My friends are getting shorter. I am not a tall woman, but I'm finding myself stooping these days to converse with some of the suddenly-short. Also, these suddenly-short are growing softer of voice. I thought it was my own fading hearing that was causing me to say an embarrassing number of *whats?* But angle-iron posture (caused by what? Spinal compression? Osteoporosis?) seems to be exacerbating their shortness. Some aging friends are becoming so round-shouldered that their words are aiming downward toward their shoes. In attempting to lip-read, I find myself sagging at the knees and then cricking my neck so I can look up at their mouths. Conversation is awkward at best, and I'm beginning to grow quite stiff.

Recently a houseguest spread his inventory of prescription medicine on our kitchen counter and began sorting pills into suites and popping them into one of those pill organizers where each cubby is marked with an initial for the different days of the week. Watching, I was reminded of the day-of-the-week underpants I wore as a little girl. When he was finished, he had a whole week's pharmacopeia compartmentalized. This is very sensible, of course, but it was unsettling to see a contemporary filling up a pill organizer for himself instead of for an elderly relative.

My friends are walking slower now. They're avoiding stairs and wondering where the elevators are. Some are walking with the rolling, side-to-side gaits common to sailors on decks and candidates for hip replacements. And the other day, I found myself discussing bariatric canes. A conversation that had started with a discussion of vertigo and balance difficulties (Meclizine was mentioned) switched abruptly to bariatric canes. I didn't even know what they were. Now I do. This can't be right! Both the prescription fellow and the one with vertigo graduated from high school in my decade.

So far my contemporaries aren't getting tight perms or blue rinses, but can those be far behind? Do not send to ask for whom the bell tolls, it tolls for thee.

OLD DAME DANCING

LOOKING UP JOHN CANDY'S NOSE

In the film *Uncle Buck,* a small boy played by McCauley Culkin is studying John Candy.

Culkin: "You have much more hair in your nose than my dad has."

Candy: "Nice of you to notice."

Culkin: "I'm a kid—that's my job."

You don't think much about nose hair during your first several decades, do you? Or ear hair for that matter. And then one day you look at someone you are fond of, someone you have known for years, and you notice great mats of hair packed into his ears. How does that happen? And when did it happen?

And what happens to legs? Guys' legs turn spindly and women's legs grow knotty, and the knees of both sexes bag. Flesh on upper arms begins to resemble cottage cheese, brown spots appear on the backs of hands, and there's a thing called ulnar drift. Want to know if you have it? Stretch your hands out in front of you and examine your index fingers. If they are torqued toward the neighboring fingers, you've got it. Yep, ulnar drift. And necks. Some necks look like something you'd find at the poultry counter. I personally know several women who have had neck work done, and I'd hate to have to say this to them, but it's hard to notice a difference. Time and money spent and pain endured and for what?

OLD DAME DANCING

I found out just the other day that hair ages. The information wasn't welcome. But right there, in an ad for a popular hair color, was the bad news along with the promise that the product could correct the seven signs of aging hair. Seven signs! I could only think of three or four. But the ad was like one of those quizzes you can't help taking. Finally, I had to go to the company's website to see all seven signs of aging hair. Here—I'll save you the trouble of looking this up. The signs are: those stubborn greys, lackluster color, coarseness, dryness, unruliness, breakage and frizzies.

Now it's discouraging enough to stand around in the privacy of your own bathroom examining these unfortunate physical manifestations, but if you have a small child in your life, your flaws go public, as John Candy found out. There is something so candid in the innocence of childish questions and observations, isn't there? Or is there? Perhaps there is real malevolence in those innocent remarks.

But you grit your teeth and answer reasonably and all the while you're thinking, "Just you wait! One of these days, oh years from now and when you're not looking, these things will sneak up on you too."

I was contemplating the garage rafters one afternoon, and muttering, when the little girl from next door materialized at my side and looked up at me. I tried not to show I was startled.

"Who are you talking to?" she wanted to know.

"I dunno. Myself, I guess."

She regarded me unblinkingly.

"Why?" she asked, "You already know what you're going to say."

Just another kid doing her job. How come kids get all the good lines?

OLD DAME DANCING

CONGENITAL DROOL

My grandmother, Mrs. Roberts, lived with us. She was in her ninth decade when I first became aware of her humorous presence, and she fascinated me. For one thing, the skin on her thin upper arms hung in soft curtains, which I liked to wobble back and forth between my hands. She was extraordinarily good-natured, and she didn't seem to mind having her flesh wobbled. I was also fascinated with the deep lines—marionette lines—that ran from the corners of her mouth toward her chin, chiefly because these were often slightly wet. Tiny rivulets of saliva tended to roll out of the corners of her mouth and these marionette lines conducted them south. She always kept a "hanky" handy to wipe up the dampness. I know. It sounds awful but somehow it wasn't.

In her 89th year, Mrs. Roberts went to her reward, which in her case meant she went to Marshall, Michigan. Marshall was a good a place for Mrs. Roberts to claim her reward. She had been born there in the 1860s, and in the 1950s it was still a pretty town, the centerpiece of the Battle Creek area, the seat of Calhoun County, and a "virtual textbook of 19th Century American architecture."

Be patient now. I'm going someplace with this.

Anyway, time passes and now my mother is showing up here, as she tends to do from time to time in this book. When she does show up, she usually appears as Maggie.

Well, Maggie had a little issue with marionette dampness also, and so she always carried about a half dozen Kleenex tissues to mop up. These she stuffed in her trouser pockets and her jacket pockets and her apron pockets, if she happened to be wearing an apron.

"I wouldn't give you a cent for anything without pockets," she always said.

She also said, "I wouldn't give you a cent for anything without nuts."

The tissues tended to bloom out of her pockets and they'd drop as Maggie heedlessly lurched on her rapid way. We could always tell where she'd been traveling though, because there was a little white trail of tissues, which my brother-in-law, who enjoyed Maggie, charitably bent over and picked up, shaking his head and chuckling as he did so.

Maggie stalked into her ninety-fifth year, strewing Kleenex as she went. Then she too, went to her reward, although she didn't go to Marshall, Michigan. She would have *liked* to go to Marshall, Michigan probably, now that I think of it. Or even to *Albion*, Michigan, where she had been born. But my sister and I rested her between our father and our Aunt Mary, who probably wouldn't have given a cent to go all the way to Michigan to claim her reward.

Still with me?

Fine. So here I am, practically in the middle of my eighth decade, and I am now discovering that the corners of my own mouth are frequently damp even though I didn't think I had really discernable marionette lines. But there they are, alright, and I am finding the need to carry around a couple of tissues in order to tidy up the corners of my own mouth from time to time.

I asked my sister, who recently blundered into *her* eighth

decade, if she had noticed this problem, and she owned up to having a little salival leakage once in a while

With this mutual admission we sat for a while, regarding each other with amusement and some irony as we clutched our Kleenex. The apple really doesn't fall far from the tree. And neither of us would give you a cent for anything without pockets.

∼

OLD DAME DANCING

STANDING ON ONE LEG

"You're standing in the middle of a roomful of people," Grace said, *"and suddenly you realize you're the oldest person there."*

Joe Coomer, Beachcombing for an Unknown God

Here I am, in the middle of my seventies, in the middle of a roomful of much younger people, and I'm standing on one leg. The other leg—the one that isn't doing the standing—is trying to do something tai chi-ish—a stretching heel kick perhaps or it's tracing little circles in mid-air with the bent knee raised. The standing leg is busy too. It's trying not to wobble.

I sometimes consider that I may be too old for this activity. Most of those standing and kicking and wobbling around me are middle-aged, although there are a couple of twenty-somethings thrown in to lower the median age and to inspire or discourage those of us who can't get our legs quite waist high. But I am not middle aged. I'm not in the middle of anything, except in the middle of my eighth decade and in the middle of a class in tai chi chaun.

In fairness, I have to say I *was* in middle age when I took up tai chi. I was in the middle of my sixth decade, as a matter fact, at a time when I thought I should improve my sense of balance in preparation for my senior years. I very quickly discovered that balance isn't really something you *learn*. Balance is a *result*. It develops through long hours and years of practice. And I found out that strength is a critical component of balance, so strength is one of the things the tai chi student works on. And then there's flexibility; that has to be developed too and that comes from stretching. Repeatedly, faithfully, sometimes painfully, the serious tai chi student bends and reaches and groans.

They say that tai chi is good for the old gourd. I agree that trying to remember the choreography of various forms is very trying for *me*.

Tai chi chaun is like golf in that you are always striving for the perfect game, the perfect performance. And like golf, perfection almost always eludes.

My tai chi classes are at night, at hours when I'd rather be wearing a fuzzy bathrobe, sitting on my tucked-up my feet and curled around a good book. Instead, I put on my practice clothes, sling my weapons bag onto my shoulder and head out into the dark of night to be humbled by the stretching, the routines, the applications, and the choreography one more time.

So here I am, wavering on one leg like a tipsy stork, considering the benefits tai chi offers and the improbability of success. And I ask myself, how long will I keep doing this? Then I consider the question's corollary, why do I do this? It's simple. I do tai chi because I can't stop doing it.

AN OLD DEAR

I hadn't seen my ophthalmologist in a while, in fact, my appointment was considerably overdue. He, of course, pointed this out, but he didn't seem to hold it against me for long.

At the end of it all, with the exam completed, the new glasses selected and measured and the bill finally paid, I extended my hand in thanks and farewell. He shook it. And then, to my surprise, he leaned forward and kissed me on the cheek, bestowing a blessing on the old girl. This is not a gesture he'd have made toward a chick, and I realized that the old dame had become an old dear.

OLD FEET

I worked with a videographer one time—this was years ago, of course—who had filmed Raquel Welch.

"Stunning woman," he told me. "Drop-dead gorgeous. Except for her feet. My camera was right at the edge of the stage so I was eye-level with her feet. She had *old* feet!"

You are filming Raquel Welch, I thought, and you are looking at her *feet*?

Then I thought about it some more. How old did her feet look, I wondered. Of course Rachel Welch's natural beauty was very well *managed*, but perhaps those managers had forgotten to include her feet. I got to thinking about this—probably longer than I should have—but I couldn't help wondering... Did her feet look her actual age? I mean, did they look like forty-five-year old feet, while the rest of her looked twenty-nine? Or did they look like seventy-five year old feet while the rest of her was only forty-five?

How old do *my* feet look these days? I've been wondering about this, but it's hard to judge the age of one's own feet. I mean, they do look old, my feet, but do they look old because the rest of me *is* old? Or do they look older than the rest of me? For instance, do they look like ninth decade feet instead of merely eighth decade feet?

I don't remember whether my mother, Maggie, had

especially old-looking feet, but I do remember her toes. She had prehensile toes. Maggie could—and did—seize and grasp objects with her toes, and then, without bending, could transfer those objects up to her hand. She instructed her daughters in the benefits of metatarsal prehensibility.

"It strengthens the arches," Maggie preached, "picking things up with your toes. Keep your feet flexible, girls."

So using our feet, we duly snatched up the socks and underpants that had fallen to the floor and tossed them jauntily aloft, snatching them right out of the air. In my eighth decade, I can still accomplish this, but it isn't a very negotiable talent, and I am not sure it contributes to the youthfulness of my feet.

I've certainly *seen* my share of old feet, and believe me, they aren't worth a second look. Lumpy. Veiny. But if feet have trod through several decades, perhaps they deserve to look old. A lot has been expected of these feet, and in the good service they've performed, they've widened, their arches have flattened, and their tendons have grown weak and loose.

Until I met that videographer, I never considered that feet might look a different age from the body on top of them. Never thought about the possible discrepancy between face and feet. I wish now that I'd pressed him for more detail about Raquel Welch's feet. If he'd had to guess, I'd like to ask him, what age would he have estimated her feet to be?

But I lost the videographer's business card long ago so the age of Raquel Welch's feet will remain forever a mystery to me. The subject is moot anyway. Whatever age her feet looked when he pointed his camera over the edge of the stage, they certainly must look a lot older now.

Or do feet get to a certain age and stop aging? Maybe they just enter a sort of stasis, waiting for the rest of the body to age and catch up with them?

I really should stop wondering.

MOTHER'S DAY: AN INCIDENT

It was Mother's Day, and I had gone out to spend the weekend with my mother.

On the eve of the holiday, we put ourselves down in the twin beds in my mother's room—the beds of my earliest memory—elegant beds of darkest mahogany, with a pineapple twist atop each of the four posts.

Sometime in the night, along toward morning I think, I heard my mother get out of bed and begin to make her way to the bathroom. This journey involved navigating the living room with its furniture, then the kitchen with its own perils, and I held my breath, waiting to hear the collision and then the fall. My muscles tensed as I prepared to spring out of bed to save her. But I reflected that my mother made this journey every night, even when I wasn't there to rescue her. Eyes open now, staring at the darkness, I lay listening.

Eventually I heard her shuffling back. I closed my eyes and faked deep breathing.

Instead of climbing into her own bed, though, she made her way across the bedroom to mine. I heard her coming.

My mother shook out the throw that was folded at the foot of my bed. She slowly spread it over me and tucked it around me, finishing with a small pat on my back. I heard her scuffle across the room to her own bed.

 She was very old. And I was old too, my own children long grown. But she was still my mother.

~

REMINDER TO MYSELF

Never miss the opportunity to lift something heavy, walk farther than is necessary, or climb an extra flight of stairs. I do this against the day when I cannot.

OLD DAME DANCING

> You're getting old when you don't care where your wife goes just as long as you don't have to go along.

IMPERFECT HARMONY

OLD DAME DANCING

MARRIAGE AND DIVINE INTERVENTION

"God watches out for marriages."

That's what my mother claimed. What she meant was, God is a matchmaker—the first *shadchan* who matched up Eve with Adam—and God is judiciously watching over couplings so no two people who are too much alike marry each other. Whenever my mother said this, we knew she was thinking about my father and Marge Shupp. In their respective houses, Marge and my father rose early and eagerly every Sunday morning to scour the real estate section in the *Cleveland Plain Dealer*. They were both on the prowl for derelict properties that could be snagged for a song and fixed up. In fact, I think Marge was the first person to cry "Location, location, location."

My mother and Marge's husband Bob Shupp had no such aspirations—in fact they had a mutual horror of the fix-er-upper, the real estate "deal", and the "needs some work" property that whispered siren songs to their spouses. Bob and my mother were always ready to rein in the enthusiasm of these spouses—ready to rain on their parades. And every time a bubble burst around one of these dream cottages, their relief was palpable.

"What if your father and Marge had gotten married?" my mother used to demand rhetorically.

"Well, I'd hate to tell you," she'd say, answering her own question. "But no. God wouldn't have allowed that. He fixes it so they couldn't have married."

She thought for a while.

"But he wouldn't have let Bob and me marry either," she decided. "If Bob and *I* had been allowed to marry, we'd probably be living in a cave and neither of us would have the gumption to move out."

To give my mother proper credit, she had reason to be wary about my father's impetuous tendencies.

One evening as we were sitting down to supper, my father said pleasantly. "I bought a house today."

While we passed around the mashed potatoes, he confided that this house was a steal; it had only cost one hundred dollars, and we'd all be taken to see it right after supper.

It was, of course, a terrible house. Its only inhabitants since the previous century had been rodents, but my father recognized it had what today is called "good bones." He planned to remove the house from its foundation and transport it to a lot he owned about five miles away, where he'd gut it and transform it into a castle.

Sighing, my mother looked on the bright side. This house would divert his interest for quite a while and the real estate section of the *Plain Dealer* would pale temporarily.

Marge was consumed with envy. She went out and got her real estate license and spent Sunday afternoons showing people around other people's houses.

Maybe it isn't actually God who does the matchmaking, but some celestial *shadchan* must be in on marriage deals, otherwise, divorce rates would be much higher than they already are.

Recently I spent some time with a half dozen old friends from high school, and the hot topic for discussion was downsizing. All of us were in our eighth decade and all of us recognized that we had too much stuff. We agreed that we really needed to weed out the crap. Even the savers said so, although they pointed out that weeding out is easier said than done. We had all plowed through the houses of deceased relatives and all of us were at the point in our lives where the thought of someone going through our stuff was sobering. We wanted to make things easier for these nieces and daughters-in-law who would be left to tidy up.

Now this is the interesting part.

There were eight of us chewing on the issue. Well, seven really because one of us was single, but among the seven marriages represented—in every case—one spouse was a saver and the other was a thrower. Gender wasn't the determining factor either. Sometimes the wife was the one who couldn't bear to throw anything away and sometimes the wife was the one who was always ready to heave stuff over the side.

Now at this point, my mother, horning into the conversation had she still be around to do it, would have piped up triumphantly. "See? Just like I said. What if both were savers? You'd have terrible hoarding situations. But no, the thrower is there to save the marriage. Or, if both were throwers, they'd end up with nothing. This way, though, there is a balance. And don't try to tell me that's not divine intervention!"

Okay, Mother, you're right. You're always right.

A MARRIAGE: 2014

It is our habit, Doyle's and mine, to sit in the evening and converse pleasantly over a cocktail while in the background (far in the background, I hope) Doyle's evening playlist unwinds through the Bose speakers. Tonight, Leo Kotke's guitar music clashes and rockets along, caroming off the very walls.

"What is he playing?" I ask, raising my voice slightly.

"*In Christ There Is No East Or West*," Doyle replies.

"It *is*?" I am incredulous. I listen to a few more bars. "It doesn't sound like the hymn I know."

"I guess it didn't sound that way to Cynthia Sears either, judging from what I heard when she played it on the organ."

"Who is Cynthia Sears?"

A look of pleasant reminiscence softens Doyle's face, carrying him back—years away—from this living room.

"Cynthia Sears invited me to watch her ride," he says. "She was working on diagonals."

"I could never figure out diagonals," I remark encouragingly. "When Liz was riding saddle seat, everyone was always leaning on the rail of the ring, talking about diagonals and, oh dear, how you were off on the wrong one...well...that's too bad, you're toast. I could never tell right from wrong."

"I couldn't tell the difference either," Doyle admits.

Another pause.

"Where were you?"

"Oh, someplace west. Lexington, I think. Or Dover. Big indoor ring, I *do* remember that."

I nod. Doyle is geographically challenged. I'd be surprised if he had known.

He picks up the narrative thread.

"When she was finished riding, she asked me if I'd like to hear her play the organ."

"Cynthia Sears."

"Yes. I told her yes."

I wait some more.

"And where did she play this organ?"

"Some church somewhere. She played this very complicated piece. Then she asked me if there was something I'd like to hear. I told her yes, I'd like to hear *In Christ There Is No East Or West*."

I swallow hard to squelch the rising hoot of laughter.

"Did she play it?"

"Yes."

"Did you like it?"

"I didn't recognize it."

"I shouldn't wonder. I mean, expecting to hear Leo Kotke's version and all. I never heard you mention Cynthia Sears. What happened to her?"

"She got married." He considers. "A short time later. To some guy," he adds helpfully.

Twenty-four years of marriage. Four or five years of getting to know each other before that. Just when you think all power to surprise has been used up or drained away, you hear about Cynthia Sears and *In Christ There Is No East Or West*.

MARRIED YOUNG

We married young in those years of the late fifties and early sixties. The statistic seems to shock—and appall—the Millennials, many of whom are still partying and dating well into their thirties. I wonder, do people still date? Or do they just go to singles bars and hang around?

I was married one month after my twentieth birthday and off I went with my new husband and his college diploma that was so fresh I feared the ink would smudge. I became a transfer student in a new university and walked to classes from our apartment complex where student-brides were common.

Our friends were other young marrieds. More or less in parallel, we moved through the stages of early married life, acquiring stereo systems, electric skillets, televisions and Danish modern furniture in matched sets—knock-offs, of course since no one could afford real Eames or Ercol. We were single-car couples, and the guys carpooled to work when one of the wives desperately needed the family car.

As we started families, the acquisition mode shifted from stereo systems to maternity dresses, cribs and infant seats. We loaned each other car seats and those infant clothes that were not too badly stained with spit-up formula and strained carrots.

By my twenty-fifth birthday my husband and I had two children, a house and a mortgage. We were frugal, shopping carefully once a week at the grocery store and pasting Green Stamps into warped-looking booklets to save for a few household luxuries. The first priority was making the mortgage payments, the second was buying Stride Rite shoes with straight lasts that would prevent our children from walking pigeon-toed when they grew up. The only cards we had were two decks of bicycle ones for the weekly bridge games that were our affordable entertainment. Our bank account was modest, but apart from the mortgage, we had no debt. After all, we were the children of Depression era parents and even the fat 50s hadn't completely obliterated our sense of thrift or the specter of future want.

Fast forward half a century. Things are different now. It's not atypical for twenty-five-year-olds to be installed in their childhood bedrooms back home with mom and dad. No kids. No mortgages. But cards? They have wallets full. For most of them, debt is practically a fact of life and family responsibilities are as foreign as Farsi. At twenty-five or thirty-five, they've never worried over a child with croup nor scrimped to buy Stride Rite shoes with straight lasts. They have probably never licked a Green Stamp, and—most tellingly—mom and dad are still referring to them as "the kids."

They're not kids. They are adults. They've just never been expected to behave that way.

So why is there such a disconnect between twenty-somethings in the 60s and the same age group in the teens of the twenty-first century? How did we end up with a generation of grown-up children?

Today's newly-minted "adults" step out into the world burdened with oppressive amounts of debt. While the cost of a college education seemed high in the 50s and 60s, compared with present costs—which are exorbitant—the figures now sound reasonable.

It seems to me that a new graduate owing thousands of dollars of college debt would be living under a cloud of discouragement.

Student loans aren't the only common debt. Credit card debt can be enormous, and once it begins to build, it reaches discouraging heights. In the credit card-free early 60s, my new husband and I simply lived off his twice-monthly paycheck and did without when we couldn't afford something.

While many Millennials feel the financial pressures of debt, there is often a sense of entitlement too. Raised with the "you deserve" ethic, indulgent parents are only too willing to grant most wishes and whims, so it's no wonder many former children are having difficulty adjusting to the idea that the world does not owe them a living.

Thus, Millennials step into the workplace, expecting to secure jobs that are interesting and never dull, jobs that pay handsomely and offer great benefits along with satisfying challenges, responsibility and respect.

"Everybody gets a trophy," sighs a contemporary of mine, as he considers the Millennial expection of praise.

The economic world in this still-young century is very different from the 60s. Avoid commitment. Enjoy your freedom. Housing costs are high and there aren't many properties to rent or buy anyway. What to do? Move home. And marriage? Who can afford that?

MEMORIES OF A MARTINI MAN

In a restaurant in 1966 the man who was then my husband took possession of a Martini with an anchovy-stuffed olive. He never got over the shock, and the experience made him deeply suspicious of all olives. Arthur was a Martini man the way some guys are leg men. Opinionated, highly specific, exquisitely detailed in specification, Martini men are never haphazard when they order.

"One Beefeater Martini, straight up and very dry with an olive on the side."

"Why on the side?" I naively asked him once.

"The olive displaces the gin," he explained patiently. "Takes up too much room in the glass and lets the bastards get away with serving less gin. After the level goes down I put the olive in myself."

See what I mean? Highly specific. A little paranoid too.

Arthur always thought someone was out to sabotage the dryness of his Martini. One night, with the vermouth bottle in hand, he was busy sneaking up on his glass of gin. He believed that only vermouth fumes produced the proper aridity, and he was just starting to wave the bottle over the glass, when our young son entered the kitchen and bumped his father slightly in passing. Just grazed his flank. Arthur screamed. The man actually screamed. A shrill yowl of pain and outrage as though the child had driven a lawnmower over his foot.

He was a purist, Arthur was. A Martini purist, but he certainly wasn't an original.

My friend Judith was a purist too. She was a PhD chemist, a responsible mother and a tireless volunteer worker in many good causes. In most things she was calm and reasonable, respected for her common sense and her uncommon organizational skills. But she refused to compromise on the dryness of a restaurant Martini and was suspicious enough to carry a hygrometer in her purse. If the specific gravity was not just right, back the Martini went!

George, a fellow Arthur and I used to play a lot of bridge with, operated on the proximity theory of dryness. George kept his gin and vermouth side by side in the refrigerator door. Arthur used to tell him that perfection demanded the catsup bottle be used as a spacer between the gin and vermouth, but that was just to get George's goat.

A man I once met at a business lunch claimed to know the Tanqueray family very well, and he insisted that the only proper Martini was served straight up, extra dry, and with a twist of orange. The acids in the orange peel, he said, brought out the botanicals in the Tanqueray recipe.

With a friend, I tested this theory once at Locke Ober's—a restaurant famous for the holiness of its Martinis. The ancient waiter absorbed our Martini order, then stared long and condescendingly at us. I think he was giving us a chance to change our minds and redeem our social standing. When we didn't flinch, he moved off to the bar. He was back in five minutes, a changed man. He was practically obsequious as he set the drinks in front of us.

"The bartender sends his compliments, sir."

(Although Locke Ober's had started admitting women to

the dining room, the waiters still didn't *talk* to them.)

"It has been years since he's had an order for a perfect Tanqueray Martini. It's a pleasure to serve you, sir."

The perfect Martini, according to my former husband, is blended reverently. I won't go so far as to say it is prayed over, but I wouldn't deny that either.

He used to consider with sorrow the abuses that Martinis have endured at the hands of amateurs, and he preached on the fragility of gin. If Arthur saw someone shaking a Martini with ice cubes, he would shudder all over as if he himself had caught a violent chill. Shaking bruises the gin, he claimed. Even vigorous stirring should be discouraged.

Besides bruising, Arthur worried about dilution. Ice was an anathema. He kept his gin in the freezer. But I have heard other purists claim freezing makes gin sluggish.

Only the best gins, according to Arthur, should be candidates for Martinis. Save your cheap gins—your house brands—for G-and-Ts. Arthur believed it was sacrilege to taint expensive gin with twice its volume of eighty-nine-cent tonic, so he drank his Beefeaters straight. Judith was partial to Boodles. Old George favored Bombay. Arthur and his friends were scandalized by blue "sapphire" gin. And the entire freemasonry agreed that ersatz Martinis made with vodka were beneath consideration.

Divided as they may be on mixing, Martini men of both sexes agree that presentation is crucial. The perfect Martini glass looks like a splayed V balanced on a stem. This is an impractical shape that requires the glass to be filled to—indeed filled above—its very rim. Then, meniscus shimmering, the Martini is transported magically to the table. The glass sweats delicately. The transparent liquid is the pure color of cold. The olive in the crotch of the glass releases its oils invisibly into the gin and absorbs into itself the gin's elixir. When such a

OLD DAME DANCING

Martini was set before him, my ex-husband's eyes shone with appreciation.

I myself have survived a Martini or two. I can drink one if I sit very still and have made no plans in the immediate future that call for the operation of machinery or the reading of a menu. It's my idea of drinking mercury—cold, slippery, with a tendency to curl in upon itself. I like the olive best.

∼

DECIDUATING

> *Junk is the stuff we throw away.*
> *Stuff is the junk we save.*
> Frank Tyger

We are in the deciduation phase, Mr. Doyle and I. This is the natural progression from the acquisition phase when young couples can't seem to get their hands on enough stuff—enough chairs to sit on, enough spoons for cereal and soup, enough ride 'em toys to keep the kids active and amused. In this first phase, the desire for stuff goes out into the ether and stuff comes flowing in like flotsam riding the tide. Eventually the tide crests and retreats and you realize you are older and you are standing on a littered beach. So one of you tells the other, "We have to get rid of some of this stuff." And you enter the deciduation phase.

Here are some of the characteristics of the deciduation phase.

1. You look around and realize you can't fit anymore stuff in.

2. You realize you're not using even half the stuff you already have. Do we really need a mandolin? Either for slicing or for playing music? And why do we still have a collection of

matchbox cars?

3. You're downsizing. Moving to an over-55 condo. In this condo you will enjoy freedom from the tyranny of lawns and gutters. Oh, but what'll we do with all that maintenance stuff? The lawnmowers and ladders, the bags of fertilizer and grass seed, the garden gloves and cans of gas for the snowblower and the half empty cans of paint?

The deciduation phase is not for the faint of heart. There are challenges.

1. The two of you can't agree on what to deciduate. (See Point 2) You argue for deciduating the matchbox cars but your spouse, who believes that stuff in collections has more value than just singular stuff—like one matchbox car—isn't ready to heave the collection over the side. So you begin the junk vs.stuff debate. (See epigram)

2. The "It's too good to throw away" argument always becomes a talking point, along with its corollary: "Somebody could use this." Hence, you've got to find this somebody. So you take trips to the Goodwill truck at every opportunity. You consider Craig's List and Freecycle. But, gosh, you paid plenty for that bookcase twenty years ago and are you ready to put it on the curb for some yo-yo to snag and probably sell at a yard sale? Hey, a yard sale. So you consider hosting a yard sale, but what happens, at the end of the day, to all the stuff that didn't sell and is now in the front yard? Stuff that has suddenly become junk. Well this is why consignment shops were invented. An interesting tactic, that, but one with its own undetonated bombs.

3. There's new stuff out there that you'd really like to have. "But we already have two televisions," one spouse points out. The other counters that one of those televisions isn't even a flat screen, which brings the whining rejoinder, "But that's the set in my den. How come it's *my* stuff you're always so

willing to trash?"

Oh, deciduating isn't easy, and it's best to start early. Like now. Better yet, like yesterday. Resolve now to stem the incoming tide. Bar the door against letting in anything new, and if you do let something in, make it a rule to delete an item that is already *in situ*. Turn, however wistfully, away from the temptation of the bright, shiny objects you see in the marketplace. In fact, it may be better to stay out of the marketplace altogether, for that is where you will see things you never dreamed you wanted or needed. But then, there they are—winkin' at ye, as the Irish say—and you suddenly recall that you always wanted a mandolin, whether for slicing or playing.

Once you've entered the deciduation phase, adopt a mantra—a charm to protect yourself against old habits developed during accumulation. *The best things in life aren't things,* you murmur a dozen times throughout the day.

The IT genius who came to cure our busted computer was wise in many ways. To him, computers weren't holy objects, they were just *things*. "It's just a piece of future junk," he told us.

Hey, isn't it all just junk?

OLD DAME DANCING

THE BATHROOM MIRROR

After my father died, my mother, Maggie, washed the spatters of his shaving soap off the bathroom mirror once and for all. She did this with a certain energy and grim satisfaction. It was the single upside to widowhood—getting rid of those spots of shaving soap that had always returned after she'd washed the mirror. They had always irritated her.

One week later, Maggie looked up at the bathroom mirror while washing her face and there they were! The shaving soap spots were back! This development gave her quite a turn.

She cast her eyes briefly toward Heaven, shivered, and washed off the spots.

A week or so later the spots were back. Maggie wondered if the mirror was haunted.

This continued for a while until one day...

"Yesterday I realized," Maggie told me, "that those shaving soap spatters that had so annoyed me, weren't caused by shaving soap at all. They were the spatters from my own toothbrushing. All those years I blamed your father..." She shook her head. "It just goes to show you."

THE GREAT CELESTIAL LOST AND FOUND

The inventory of The Great Celestial Lost and Found includes my husband's navy blue Guernsey sweater and a practically-new pair of Mudrucker barn boots.

"How could you lose a pair of boots?" I demanded to know.

"I dunno. I had them when I went on the hike last Wednesday."

"That's my point," I persisted. "They were on your *feet*, right? You didn't come home in your stocking feet, surely. You'd have remembered that."

He allowed that it was a great mystery and one for which he had no answer, although he'd looked high and low and even phoned my sister out in Belchertown to ask if they had an unclaimed pair of barn boots in their back hall, size 10. They didn't. They just had their own barn boots.

I'd like to get a look at The Great Celestial Lost and Found. It must be chock-a-block full of the most amazing things, besides my husband's good woolen Guernsey and the usual, run-of-the-mill lost things—the orphaned socks, the limp mittens, the widowed gloves—that disappear at the end of winter. I'll bet I'd find a few items that I've been missing.

My Foley food mill, for one thing. Given its awkward shape, it's difficult to misplace, maddening to store, and I can't think what I would have done with it.

The Great Celestial Lost and Found is where objects automatically go when people put them down on the roofs of cars for just a second while they do one other thing and then off they drive, forgetting about the object on the roof and bingo—it sails off into The Great Celestial Lost and Found.

The Great Celestial Lost and Found probably has entire sections reserved for cell phones and car keys and sunglasses and other areas reserved for hooded sweatshirts and half-used tubes of ChapStick. Umbrellas! That's another one, and goodness, there could be an entire warehouse dedicated to umbrellas. And this warehouse, is it organized into sections, do you imagine? Or do you think stuff just gets chucked in there so all the lost stuff gets mixed up in a huge celestial landfill of junk?

For a while my husband swore our tree saw was in The Great Celestial Lost and Found. No, that's not right. I thought that's where it was; he thought someone had pinched it.

"Just went into our garage in search of a tree saw and took ours?" I said sarcastically. "Or do you think the thief wandered in casually for no real reason, saw the tree saw, and said ah-ha! The very thing?"

"It doesn't matter," Doyle said bitterly. "Now the tree saw is gone, and I think some guy took it."

I went to the hardware store and bought a new tree saw. A yellow one. Six months later the original tree saw—the red one—was back, hanging on the designated nail with the new yellow one.

"He brought it back!" Doyle exclaimed. "The thief brought it back. Both of us looked at that nail a dozen times and the saw definitely wasn't there, and now it's back."

It was a mystery to me too, and one that confirmed my belief in The Great Celestial Lost and Found. The guy in charge of the place—I don't know who, the angel or the celestial dump manager or whomever—probably said to himself, "What's this thing doing here?" and he zapped the tree saw back to the nail in the garage. And I wish he'd zap back those Mudrucker boots because a new pair will cost a hundred bucks plus the gas for an inconvenient trip up to the Essex Agricultural Co-op to buy them. So I haven't made the trip up there yet. I'm still waiting.

OLD DAME DANCING

WHAT IF I WERE A WITNESS?

"What if I witnessed a murder?" I thought as I reeled out of the bathroom and left the plumber to the business of reconstructing the shower mechanism. "My testimony would be worthless."

The plumber's question was a simple one. He asked it as he stood there with the shower handle in his hand.

"Was this handle originally installed up or down?"

Now I'd been operating that handle on a daily basis for twenty years, but I was stumped. I had no idea. Seeing the vacant look on my face, the plumber tried to help me out.

"Did the hot water come out first? Or did you first get cold water when you turned the handle?"

I still had no idea, and his question further confused me.

"I...I'm not sure."

I heard reinforcements coming up the stairs, and I fell upon my husband as the wolf on the fold.

"Come in here," I ordered, pulling on his bicep.

The plumber, looking relieved, repeated his question. Mr. Doyle didn't know the answer either.

"Just install it the way you want," I gabbled. "It'll be fine what ever you do."

The plumber looked unhappy, but Mr. Doyle supported me.

"Yes," he said, "just put it in the way you think it should work best. We'll learn to operate it however it ends up."

Doyle and I fled, and I hurried down the stairs ahead of him so as to be the one further away in case the plumber thought of another challenging question. And fleeing, I thought of the witness issue. If I couldn't even remember which way my own faucet turned—an object I'd seen and used every day—how could my testimony be accurate if I were called to testify to something I'd seen that was *really* important—an accident or, god forbid, a vicious crime?

Is it that we take the small things of our lives so much for granted? Or are Doyle and I unusually dim?

The plumber finished his work and went away with our check. Mr. Doyle and I climbed the stairs and inspected his work. We stared at the handle.

"Is this the way it used to be?"

"I can't remember."

For the better part of the day, this failure troubled me. But I am pretty sure that when one or the other of us steps into the shower and turns that handle, we will remember. It is muscle memory that drives the hundreds of small, rote movements we make in a single day—the depressing of the clutch, the tying up of a trash can liner, the direction you turn the key to lock the door, the screwing in of a light bulb, the release of the electric mixer's bowl. I can do all these things, but don't ask me how.

OLD DAME DANCING

WHEN A HUSBAND RETIRES

He'd planned to work three years longer, but the job grew increasingly impossible. Responsibilities increased but the compensation did not. He was juggling a job that had formerly been handled by three people, and he'd had it. He gave his two-week notice and stood his ground when they tried to argue him out of it. He trained a recruit. He shook hands all around and came home. Then the doubt set in.

Had he jumped too soon? And who was he now—now that he wasn't who he had been?

Some of us—men especially—seem to derive our identities from our occupations and professions, and when those are stripped away, there can be confusion and a horrible sense of vulnerability. This must be the way a lobster feels when it sheds its shell and creeps away to hide under a rock until it grows a new carapace of protection.

For a few days there was euphoria. Then the fog of ennui set in. He watched the dog and me start out for our routine walk and wondered if he could come too. Was I going to the grocery store? Yes, was there something I could get for him? No, but he'd be pleased to come along.

There was panic in his eyes. I understood. I tried to be patient, but I was feeling brushes of panic too. Was this how it was going to be from now on? Were we destined to act out some marital version of conjoined twins?

Then I remembered one of the lessons of Louis Randa, the founder of the Peace Abbey and The Life Experience School. Louis tried to teach the school's special needs children to be open to new things. Being "available" he called it.

I once heard him tell a story that went something like this: He, Louis, was driving the school's van full of children, and they came to a four-way stop. Louis stopped, looked, then cautiously accelerated. An oncoming car did not stop, and it plowed into the side of the van. Louis described how the ensuing seconds elongated as time extruded into slow motion. Terrified, he turned slowly to look at his passengers. Every single child was sitting bolt upright in a seat, looking forward at the teacher with complete calm and even a certain eagerness. Then, into the reverberating silence that follows such a crash, one child spoke up.

"We're available."

When I retired, a dozen years before my husband, I had vowed to be like a child of the Life Experience School. I would be available. And after I left my office in the advertising agency for good, opportunities undreamed started to me. All I had to do was say yes to them.

So I gave my Louis Randa "be available" speech to my husband.

Shortly after that, Mr. Doyle was working at the library book sale with a man he knew only slightly, but the fellow grew quite animated when he heard of the retirement.

"Then you must walk with us on Wednesdays," he declared. He was so enthusiastic and Mr. Doyle was so desperate, that they made a date. Doyle returned from that walk looking radiant. A naturalist had guided them through the woods; they'd seen a beaver lodge and an old soapstone quarry. He'd met congenial people, and he was going back the following Wednesday. That was two years ago and he has never since missed a Wednesday morning walk.

In the years since, he has accepted positions various boards of the church and town. He has displayed his paintings and judged art shows, given speeches and become something of an expert on the town's history.

Being available means saying yes when opportunities come along. New things. Things undreamed of. It means kicking aside original reservations, moving out of your comfort zone, and being brave. And who knows? You may meet with success unexpected in common hours.

If you gotta ask, you'll never know
Louis Armstrong,
asked to explain jazz

ANSWERS TO QUESTIONS NOBODY ASKED

OLD DAME DANCING

OLD DAME DANCING

WHY KATHARINE HEPBURN WORE TURTLENECKS

I guess I'm just a turtleneck kind of girl
Diane Keaton to Jack Nicholson
in Something's Gotta Give

In her later years, Katharine Hepburn never appeared in a movie or an interview—or in public either, for that matter—without being swathed to her famous jawline in some kind of garment—a scarf perhaps, but most of the time a turtleneck. When I was younger, I figured she was cold. Now I think she was just covering up her neck.

I didn't think much about necks—Hepburn's or anyone else's—until my friend Pat raised my consciousness about them. After that, I've hardly thought about anything else. Pat had discovered her husband was having an affair with her best friend Corinne and the resulting divorce was protracted, acrimonious and just plain messy. I know because I heard about every vicious bit of it from Pat. Things got settled though. Eventually. But then time passed and Pat found herself headed back to court to grizzle with her ex over an issue of child support or alimony or something, and this required that Pat haul herself into a pair of pantyhose and a skirt and go off to court.

Naturally I wanted to know how it went and at my first opportunity, I asked.

"It was wonderful," she replied. "Corinne was there. Her neck has died."

I tried to imagine it. I hadn't known necks could die. So while I was still in my 'forties, I started examining my own neck with some regularity, looking for signs of its demise. And while I'm sorry to have to confess this, I also started scrutinizing the necks of my friends. Yes, I apologize, ladies, but once you know a thing you can't "unknow" it, and after Pat gave me the facts of neck life—well, I've be going to private little funerals for necks I once knew as slender, smooth and swanlike.

And how about those pads of fat at the *backs* of necks! Have you noticed those? That's another dandy little age signature, isn't it? Dorsocervical fat pads, those are called. I looked it up. Also buffalo hump. Usually terribly thin people don't have buffalo humps, proof that a really scrawny neck sometimes buys immunity from the fat pad issue, although not necessarily immunity from osteoporosis and chicken necks.

Chicken necks are different than turkey necks. A chicken neck is scrawny but a turkey neck is fancier, featuring relapsed material that used to be on the jaw and chin but has fallen into wattles.

But what are we supposed to do about necks? Katharine Hepburn dressed hers up and it was called radical chic. Other women get neck lifts. I complained about my neck once to a friend and she started trying to sell me on a neck job. It's very simple she told me, although I didn't believe her for a minute. You simply get a shot of anesthesia and some surgeon pins your surplus neck skin up around your ears. I've seen a couple of neck jobs worn by people who claim to be very happy with them, and to tell the truth, I've never seen much difference between the befores and afters.

But what am I going to do about my neck? Simply try to get over its death, I guess, and take the Hepburn approach, invest in scarfs and turtlenecks and aim for radical chic.

OLD DAME DANCING

WHY I HATE TO TRAVEL

*Why do the wrong people travel travel travel
When the right people stay back home?*
Noel Coward

I have eight easy answers.

Airplanes. Of course nobody likes airplanes any more, and here are some of the reasons why: lines, rates, weather delays in Chicago, TSA rules, TSA searches, TSA *people*, taking off your shoes, standing around in stocking feet, lack of leg room in plane cabins, other passengers, overhead compartments, debris in the seat from the previous flight, stale cabin air, getting to airports, reclining seats in front of you, 3.4 ounce bottles of anything, waiting, crying kids, armrest pirates, getting knocked in the head by other people's bags, RFID, people who break the one-carry-on-bag-per-passenger rule, landing, taking off ... don't get me started.

Suitcases. I still haven't found the perfect suitcase. The perfect bag will be commodious enough to hold all the things I will need on my trip, but at the same time it will be compact enough to glide under an airplane seat and lightweight enough for me to carry down concourses without tipping to one side and holding out the other arm for ballast. It will be black so it won't show dirt, but at the same time it won't be black because if it's black, I won't be able to find anything inside it. It must be a carry-on because I don't like to check my bag, and if I *did* check my bag, the list under Airplanes would have a subcategory called "Baggage, checking of" and the list of reasons I hate to travel would be much, much longer.

Packing. There is so much compromising connected with packing. No matter how cannily I pack (and I really work at this) I never seem to have what I need or want or else I *do* have it and just can't find it. (See previous note on Black Bag, Interior). Shoes are one of the main problems. The shoes that you wore all day to hike around Manhattan aren't going to "go" with the silk dress you're wearing to dinner. And then there's rain gear. Even my scrunchable, roll-it-into-a-ball rainwear takes up room in the suitcase. A pair of extra shoes and that raingear and that's about all the carryon bag will hold

Beds other than my own. There are a lot of Three Bears beds out there—either too hard or too soft. Same goes for pillows. I don't like pillows that fight back. My bed at home is firm with a down mattress on top. It is just the right height for dismounting. The headboard is high and rigid so I can lean against it and read, and the lamp over my left shoulder is of the perfect angle and brightness for reading in bed. The bedside table is within easy reach and has plenty of room for my book, my spectacles, the clock and the water glass.

Bathrooms other than my own. Sometimes you draw a good one in the bathroom lottery, but you can't depend on getting one with enough room on the sink to hold your accouterments. You can't be sure of drawing a bathroom with a good mirror that is close enough for a nearsighted person to lean toward comfortably and one with excellent lighting so that the nearsighted person can see what she's up to when she leans toward the mirror. Toilet heights matter (see above comment on beds). And cleanliness—well, I always wonder, don't you?

OLD DAME DANCING

Leaving home. Did we leave the light on? The stove? How 'bout the iron—you unpluged it, didn't you? What do you mean, you don't remember? Did we tell the neighbors we were going and ask them to take in the mail and the trash cans? Did we leave our cell phone numbers with the boarding kennel? I'm already starting to miss my own coffeepot.

Returning home. The house looks dim and everything looks faded and that's when you discover A) you left the coffee grounds in the filter in the pot B) the mail the neighbors left on the counter includes some very unattractive bills C) the answering machine readout is pulsating with messages from people you don't want to hear from, telling you things you don't want to know; this includes, but is not limited to, political messages and solicitations from charities. D) why didn't you ever notice the three-corner tear in the upholstery on the wing chair?

Having people tell me why I need to travel. People who like to travel, try to convince me that I would like it too if I would just for heaven's sakes *try*. Travel would be *good* for me. These proponents of travel are prepared to argue long and persuasively that I Will Love It and they don't abandon their arguments easily. I won't love it for a number of reasons (see above). Moreover, the times I have traveled have been relatively disastrous. My phone credit card was compromised in the Dallas-Fort Worth airport and I got a bill for $6,749 after I got home. When we went to Florida, the pet sitter and her husband had to move out of their own house and into ours into because the dog was too nervous to stay in an unfamiliar house. She expressed her distress with an extreme case of diarrhea. We received a phone call 36 hours after arriving in Northern California wine country—the same dog had been stricken with something terminal and the veterinarian was trying to keep her alive until we got home. We called the airport, paid a premium to change our tickets and flew home to New England. The dog held on until we got there. On that same trip, although I didn't know it at the time, my husband became convinced that the altitude and cabin pressure would cause his lung to collapse; therefore he endured long hours of paranoid anguish. His lung did collapse a short time later, so his concern was not unfounded, but we were safely on the ground when it did. We haven't left the ground since. We don't plan to.

∼

OLD DAME DANCING

WHY WE'RE STILL HERE

*And when we are in the place just right
We will be in the valley of love and delight*
Shaker hymn

Starter home ... downsizing ... empty nesters ... nobody used these terms in the era of bouffant hair and flared polyester pants when my first husband and I moved into our pleasant Cape Cod cottage on a dead-end street. The house—a "soldier's house"—had been built just after the war when returning G.I.s had an acute need for housing and when plats of modest homes were being hastily constructed. Ours included. The house, like its neighbors, has gone through a number of face-lifts, remodels and add-ons and has, I've always thought, a certain low-key charm, but I never really thought of it as a starter home. Not until last week.

Last week I pushed my market basket abreast of the basket of a friend whom I hadn't seen in a dog's age. Cued by my question, "What's new with you?" she actually started telling me. She'd been in Alaska. Or maybe it was the Aleutians. The Galapagos was mentioned. She had seen amazing sights. She told me about each one. Meanwhile, her sister in Minneapolis had been in the hospital with a gall bladder thing that led to complications. She described these. I was starting to worry that the frozen turkey breast in my market basket would defrost, but finally she wound it all up by telling me that her niece's family had moved into a starter home in a quiet neighborhood. "Much like yours," she told me. "Not that yours is a *starter* home," she added hastily. "I mean, it's *lovely*, it's just that ... just that..."

"I know what you mean," I cut in soothingly. And I did. And what she meant was that we hadn't moved with the times. Moved up and moved out, as Billy Joel might phrase it. We were stuck in the mud of a modest little house—well, hovel really—where the old saw "be it ever so humble" definitely applied.

That revealing conversation got me thinking. Apparently I've been living for more than forty-five years in a starter home, and now that the only thing I'm starting is advanced old age, I have to ask myself, *why* am I still living in a starter home? Why did I never upsize? Why did I never move on, move out, move up, as apparently I was expected to do? Here's why.

We never got around to it, that's why. Life just got in the way. We were doing other things. We never noticed we were still here.

Then too, there were reversals of fortune. Times when we would have been laughed out of a bank had we been reckless enough to apply for a larger mortgage. Those were the years my then-husband folded all our assets into a tropical fish store. Don't get me started on that!

I bought out his half of the house when we divorced, which happened during a real estate bubble; house prices were enormously inflated and interest rates were at nose-bleed heights. Same address; heftier mortgage.

Eventually, when another husband joined me and we'd become a family, we stayed because we were happy here.

Content. Comfortable. We never envied nor longed for fancier, larger digs. Where else would we find such a pleasant quality of life?

Oh, but the house has history. Two small children grew up here, eventually outgrowing their childhoods. Six dogs have been licensed here (not simultaneously, thank goodness). There's been a cat, birds, tanks of tropical fish, rabbits and hamsters. I don't know how many hamsters. I don't ever want to know how many hamsters.

Time sifted it all out. The boy's room became a guestroom. I moved my office out of the closet in the upstairs hall and into the girl's former room. The guestroom became my new husband's dressing room. The cellar transmogrified into an art studio. With the addition of a comfortable chair, a good reading lamp and a solid wall of books, the dining room doubled as a library.

Now here I am in my eighth decade, and we've never sent out change of address cards and have no immediate plans to do so. A number of people we know—upwardly mobile, empty-nesters who left their starter homes—now speak wistfully of downsizing. Of moving back to something like the first homes they couldn't wait to leave. And Mr. Doyle and I are finding things are coming full circle and that we have been—all along—in the place just right.

∼

OLD DAME DANCING

WHY I'M AILUROPHOBIC*

I am not comfortable around cats. I actually lived with a cat for 18 years and I wasn't comfortable the whole time and neither was she. The troubling thing is, most cats seem to like me. When I visit a house with a resident cat—or cats (people seem to have them in plurals)—the cat looks me over. And as I am being sized up, I start to feel uncomfortable.

"Ha!" the cat figures, "I'll have the upper hand with this one."

And before long, it sidles up to me and insinuates itself back and forth against my legs. Or it hops up on the arm of my chair, settles in, and commences to stare at close range. After a while the power of this unrelenting scrutiny distracts me to the point of losing the thread of the conversation I've been having with the cat's owner. I've tried staring back at the animal, but I can't hold out. In staring contests, the cat always wins. They have an infinite number of resources, cats. I don't think they blink. At any rate, I've never seen a cat blink.

Here's another thing about visiting homes with cats.

At some point during the visit, the cat(s) will jump onto the kitchen counter or the dining room table that is all set for dinner. The cat owner is horrified. He/she jumps up also, and loudly scolds the offending cat. The cat gives the owner an insolent look that clearly accuses him/her of hypocrisy. At this point, the animal usually drops down from the counter or table and saunters off with the attitude of I'm not going because you told me to, I'm leaving because I damn well feel like it. My apologetic host returns; he/she is aghast. I am supposed to infer that the cat's transgression is highly unusual. I am not fooled. That cat is up on the kitchen counter several times each and every day, and when the table is all dolled up for dinner guests, well, the cat feels entitled—even feels it is necessary, its hostly duty perhaps—to inspect the table. It must swerve in and out among the wine glasses and water goblets. It must lean over and sample the fresh flowers in the centerpiece. I, watching surreptitiously, think of the litter box where those four paws have so recently been. And I am not duped by the owner's feigned surprise and outrage. If I weren't here, the cat would simply earn a casual swat and a "Bad Kitty. Get down."

My sister was taking care of a neighbor's cat when she—my sister herself—was called away. She convinced me to go to the neighbor's house twice a day to feed the cat. She gave me all the necessary instructions.

"And oh by the way..." she said.

[Now here I'm going to explain that 'oh by the way' is a phrase that sets off all alarms and bells for me.]

"Oh by the way," she said. "Stand on a chair while you feed her."

"Stand on a chair? Why?"

"Because her tail got cut off accidently and it isn't quite healed. When you're making her dinner, she rubs back and forth against your legs and the scab feels funny."

So I stood on a chair and cranked open the cans of cat food, and I listened to the plaintive meows beneath the chair and wondered how I'd gotten into this position.

When I am visiting a house with a resident cat for the first time, my hostess usually asks, "Do you mind cats?"

And I'm in a big hurry to lie. "Oh no," I say, "I *like* cats."

Once in a while the owner will apologize for her cat. "He doesn't like strangers," she'll say sadly, while the cat, clearly offended that its home has been invaded, stalks off to some dim sanctuary to sulk until I leave. These are cats I actually like.

But in houses where the cat doesn't mind strangers, where the animal boldly sits in meatloaf position, evaluating guests, I become a little anxious. I can see it plotting and biding its time. So with a lie, I have opened myself to what is bound to happen during the visit. I have made myself vulnerable to the staring match or to the back-and-forth rubbing or even to the secretive claw swipe to the ankle that comes undercover of the tablecloth when everyone is seated for dinner.

Yes, this is my fault, and I should summon up the crust to tell another sort of lie.

"Actually," I could say, "I *like* cats but I am extremely allergic to them."

Then I'd paste on an apologetic and rueful smile, while the embarrassed owner scurries around, rounding up her felines to shut them away in some bedroom far from the kitchen counter or the dining table. Whew. Now I can concentrate on conversation.

*Fear of cats

~

WHY WE DINE ON THE FLOOR

Mr. Doyle and I met when we were both sitting cross-legged on a floor. Well, actually we didn't meet until we'd gotten up off the floor at the end of the meeting when everyone was supposed to mingle and get to know one another. That's when we met. By the guacamole dip. There was a lot we didn't know about each other at that point, except that we both liked guacamole dip. We didn't know, for example, that we each spent a lot of time sitting on floors. I mean, not just at meetings where there weren't enough chairs to go around and where both of us tended to charitably volunteer to sit on the floor.

Mr. Doyle, an artist, had installed his enormous drawing board quite close to the floor in his apartment, and he spent hours, sitting like an old-fashioned tailor, working at the board. His sartorius muscles were nothing short of remarkable.

Meanwhile, in the defensive tactic of the single parent (I wasn't really single at that point, but my husband was never home in the evenings) I had discovered the best method for waylaying arguments between my children at the dinner table was to by-pass the dinner table altogether and serve the evening meal on low TV trays in front of the set. I am not proud of this. I cite exhaustion.

OLD DAME DANCING

Fast-forward to the present. We—Mr. Doyle and I—have a regulation dining room. In its center is a fine, round table. We sit cross-legged on the floor in a whole other room, happily dining at a pair of low antique tables set side by side. I recommend this. In this eightieth decade we can both stand up in one smooth try without hauling our bodies up with the aid of a piece of furniture; moreover, we can both drop into the cross-leg position with the ease of eight-year-olds. It's all in the practice.

You should try it. Well ... perhaps it's too late. You should have.

> *"In my youth," said the sage, as he shook his grey locks,*
> *I kept all of my limbs very supple*
> *By the use of this ointment—one shilling the box—*
> *Allow me to sell you a couple?"*
> *Father William Lewis Carroll*

∼

OLD DAME DANCING

*A writer writes as long as he lives.
It is the same as breathing,
except it is bad for one's health.*
 E.B. White

OLD DAME WRITING

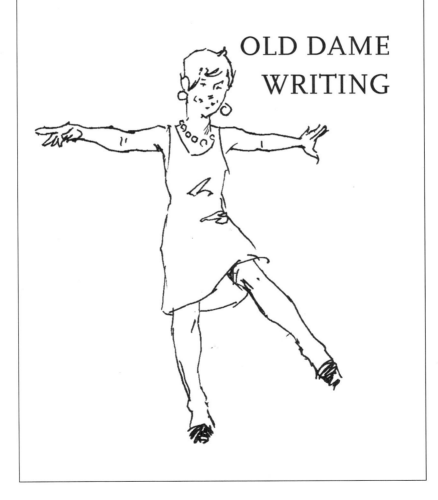

OLD DAME DANCING

OLD DAME WRITING

I have made my living writing. I figure I've written everything except poetry and pornography. Here's the list:
Juveniles
Plays
Remedial reading material
Business letters for myself
Business letters for other people
Short fiction for magazines
Humor
How-to articles
Technical white papers
Trifold brochure copy
Advertisements for national magazines
Memoirs
Novels
Facility brochures
Press releases
Obituaries
Eulogies
Sympathy letters
Congratulatory letters

Catalog copy
Newspaper articles
Financial documents
Technical documents
Video scripts
Full length, non-fiction books

* * *

Much of this writing was done in the employ of other people. People who didn't want to do the writing themselves, or who couldn't, and so were willing to hire a professional pen—well, word processor—fortunately mine. Somehow I earned enough to make a modest living and send two kids to through college.

Those kids were very small when I began this curious occupation. The best time to write was early in the morning before they woke up. So I rose at four-thirty and stumbled to the kitchen where my Brothers portable typewriter sat on a sharp-edged metal utility table in a corner of the breakfast nook. The first sleepy child to arrive in the kitchen ended the day's writing, and I was too sleepy myself to write at night.

I can observe my writing process through the machines I wrote on. An IBM Selectric (second-hand) took over from the Brothers, and then an IBM PC Jr. obsoleted the Selectric.

Eventually there was a new house, and I had a writing room ... well, a writing closet. Still had the same utility table though. It was shoved into the closet under a low eve and the PC Jr. was illuminated shakily by a pin-up lamp with a trailing cord.

We were snowbound for a week in the Blizzard of '78 and that was fortunate because I had accepted a job to rewrite a thick educational manual—a tedious piece of business full of unfamiliar, educational jargon. In my opinion, the manual needed more than a rewrite; it needed a burial at sea. And I, at sea myself, rode out the blizzard trying to rewrite the damned thing.

The PC Jr. evolved into a graduating series of senior PCs, more of them than I can recall. I wrote with Bill Gates at my elbow, whispering annoying suggestions and disapproving of my word choices. Then Bill and I parted ways, and I took up with Steve Jobs and now write on a whisper-silent iMac.

In my eighth decade, I'm still here. Still writing. Possibly because this is a profession that doesn't wear out your knees. Roofing contractors, baseball catchers, shoe salesmen, they all retire young and have to find something else to do, like sitting in leather lounge chairs watching sports on TV. My fingers are still nimble; of course it helps that I no longer have to strike those heavy keys of a manual typewriter. I still rise early to write, but not at four-thirty AM.

I still like ghostwriting. The checks still cash.

OLD DAME DANCING

GHOSTWRITERS IN THE SKY

With apologies to Frankie Laine, Johnny Cash, Judy Collins, and their galloping renditions of Ghost Riders In The Sky

A ghostwriter went ridin' out one dark and windy day.
Upon a ridge she rested as she went along her way,
When all at once a mighty herd of red-bound books she saw
A flyin' through the ragged skies and up a cloudy draw
    "Lordy, no way-ay ... Deadline's today!"
    Ghostwriters in-n-n the sky

Their pages were on fire and their covers made of steel.
Their type was black and shiny and their hot breath she could feel.
A bolt of fear went through her as they thundered through the sky.
Then she saw the writers comin' hard and she heard their mournful cry
    "Lordy, no way-ay ... Deadline's today!"
    Ghostwriters in the sky

Their faces gaunt, their eyes were blurred, their shirts were soaked with sweat.

They're writin' hard to make their date but they ain't made it yet.
On keyboards hot as fire while their tired fingers fly,
Tryin' to chase that perfect word
Across that endless sky.
    "Lordy, no way-ay ... Deadline's today!"
    Ghostwriters in the sky

The writers roared on by her, and she heard one call her name,
"If you want to save your soul from hell a writin' on our range,
Then girlfriend change your ways today or with us you will write
Tryin' to catch the book deadlines a-cross this endless night.
    "Lordy, no way-ay ... Deadline's today!"
    Ghostwriters in the sky
    Ghostwriters in the sky
    Ghostwriters in the sky

∼

I'LL MISS NELL BANE

Nell Bane arrived in my life during a walk in the park. Jack, my intense terrier, was busy reading pee mail and leaving his own business cards for other dogs to read, and at the north end of the leash, I was conducting business of my own. My business that morning was to invent the central character in my next novel. This character had to be appealing, I'd decided, especially to me. Therefore the character would have to be versatile enough to reappear in each book I intended to write. Moreover, I didn't want to write steamy sex scenes or use the raunchy language that seems practically essential in fiction today. Ethics, psychology and intrigue, I decided, would be the common denominator throughout the series. I was aiming for a Robert B. Parker meets Rosamund Pilcher tone.

Then here she came, Nell Bane. It was as if my astral body had stepped outside myself and begun walking alongside. I'm not sure I recognized her right away. Readers did though—at least the readers who knew Nell Bane's creator. So perhaps I was among the last to recognize Nell as my alter ego.

Nell Bane is a woman of mature years, although not quite so mature as mine. She is a small figure with short, wispy white hair, dry skin and a dry wit. Personally, I don't have dry skin and I have no hair at all, so as you can see, Nell and I are not twins.

We had a good time together, Nell and I. A good run. And during the running time, we traveled to Manhattan and Beacon Hill. We got to live in Newburyport, Massachusetts, close to a wonderful psychotherapist-turned-potter named Bunty Whitney. We went to the Suffolk Superior Court for Criminal Justice in Boston and to the Peabody Essex Museum in Salem. Together, we re-experienced childhood on Squam Lake and explored the history of the Swift River Valley.

Nell Bane was granted some of the things I've always wanted and will probably never have, namely an Aga—a British cooker on which to simmer soup. Soup recipes feature in all the Nell Bane books. The recipes came about this way, and right here I'll invite my friend Karen into the essay to explain.

One Saturday afternoon during National Novel Writing Month, Karen and I were sitting quietly in the library, each diligently working our way toward the last counted word in our 50,000-word novels. After a while, we took a short break and compared a few notes.

Karen had a confession. "I'm putting recipes in my book," she whispered. "You know, to use up words."

She looked sort of guilty.

I was amazed.

"I'm doing the same thing," I exclaimed. "My character makes soup."

Karen's heroine was a baker, and when her novel was published, I read it and got the most delicious cookie recipe ever. Karen and I did an author's program together to introduce our books and all the refreshments were made from the recipes in Karen's novel.

The fifth Nell Bane novel was the last. Originally I intended to write three books. Then the National Novel writing challenge came around again, and I, snorting like an old fire horse, plunged out of the barn once more and started galloping into a fourth book—*The Ghost Paints A Portrait*. But I was terribly uncomfortable with an even-numbered series. Convinced that an uneven number was necessary, I began the last novel—*The Ghost Lays The Ghosts To Rest*. It is, right now, my favorite Nell Bane book. And wishing to carry Nell out on a high note, I decreed, the series would end. I didn't want to risk becoming overly formulaic. I didn't want to wear out Nell's welcome.

But I will miss Nell Bane. She taught me that novel writing is fun. I, the writer, was constantly wondering—as I hoped my readers might—what would happen next. While I had general ideas, I often didn't know what was going on until my fingers, operating on the keyboard seemingly of their own volition, revealed plot and character, somehow reaching back into the draft to pluck up threads and references that I didn't consciously seek and thus weave them into the structure of the novel.

As I laid the ghosts to rest, I rested my short career as a novelist and returned to my former place as a ghostwriter and a writer of non-fiction.

We returned to our places, these Kingdoms," wrote T.S. Eliot, *"But no longer at ease here, in the old dispensation.*

A dispensation, so I am informed—at least in the Christian sense—is a distinctive arrangement that forms the framework through which God relates to mankind. So perhaps the novel-writing experience was simply a gift of grace. If so, I am grateful for the gift.

IRISH THUNDER

Irish Thunder: The Life and Hard Times Of Micky Ward is the current book on my bedside table. It's the story of a hardscrabble boxer from Lowell, Massachusetts, and maybe it sounds like an unusual reading choice for an old dame like me. Well, I bought the book because I admired the writing style of its author, Bob Halloran. Halloran is a sports reporter for Boston's WCVB-Channel 5 news, and every time Bob shows up on the TV screen, my writer's ear catches a style that is distinctive. Witty. Beautifully balanced, and completely different from the run-of-the-mill reporting that usually drones out of the TV, be it sports or weather or accounts of the current outrages and atrocities that among the news media, passes for stirring reporting. Style, that's what Halloran's reports have. And voice—that ineffable sound that catches you, makes you listen. Voice, that's the thing. It's the voice. I knew Halloran had written a book, and I went searching for it. *Irish Thunder* didn't disappoint. From the first, splendidly balanced paragraph, it had me.

A dozen bellies cozy up to the bar. Shots and beers for a small group of men. It's nine o'clock in the morning, and drinking seems like a good idea. It had been this way at the Highland Tap for the better part of three decades, and if it stayed that way for three more, that would suit these men just fine.

It's a paragraph worthy of James Joyce—a distant echo straight from Blazes Boylan's deep Dublin den. Do other people hear it, that music?

It's on the first page of *Cannery Row*. It's in Molly Bloom's soliloquy. In F. Scott Fitzgerald's description of Gatsby's party. It's in any book, essay, letter, interoffice memo or single sentence written by E.B. White.

How is it that a compelling writing style can so powerfully draw a reader through a long account of a life in a sport so alien as boxing?

It's simple. The words don't necessarily matter. We read for the music. We read for the pure beauty of it.

∼

GRACE DURRIN OF TROUP STREET

The stretch of Route 6 that slices through Bowling Green in northwestern Ohio is known locally as E. Wooster St., and during the reign of Grace Durrin, it marked the southern boundary of Bowling Green State University. Below Route 6 was a dense plat of bungalows and side streets—Troup Street among them. By now, I suppose, the university has overflowed its banks and swamped the neighborhood, including Troup Street, but it doesn't matter, because I am long gone from Bowling Green and so is Grace Durrin.

In the spring semester of my freshman year, I was just beginning my writing career and Grace was just ending hers.

Expository writing 201 was an elective, and I elected it, bracing myself against the reputation of its ferocious professor, Grace "Hell on Wheels" Durrin—a reputation so infamous on campus, that all you had to say was "Grace" and people shuddered.

The door to her classroom was at the rear, and she'd charge through this door at precisely one minute past the hour, traveling at warp-speed with her high heels punishing the wood floor. She was a handsome woman, somewhere up in her seventies. Her white hair was upswept. Her pleated skirts perfectly matched her cashmere sweaters, and the velocity at which she traveled caused those pleats to swish from side to side. In much the way a terrier leans into his harness, anticipating the snap that will kill the rat, she drove herself forward, propelled by an anticipation to get to the front of the classroom and begin teaching.

Her shoulders sagged under the weight of the inevitable stack of books required as reference during her lessons. Slam down on the desk went the books, and Grace started teaching expository writing 201 with all her might and main. Lecturing, she yanked books from the stack and whiffled impatiently through them until she found the example she wished to cite. When she found it, she relaxed in pleasure, her rapid-fire speech slowed, and the writer's words were given the respectfully round tones each syllable deserved. She gave each word to her young students the way a precious gift is given, and when the reading was finished, *slam*! went the book, and Grace "Hell on Wheels" Durrin resumed her fire-hose delivery.

She loved good writing. That was evident to each of us. And plainly, she didn't see enough of it. That was our fault. Lord knows, she tried to cadge good writing out of us, but she must have ended most days in despair. If that were true, it didn't daunt her. The next day she was ready again—ready to roll the boulder up the hill. In optimism, she assigned essay after essay, only to have hope snuffed out as she sat evenings in her house at 116 Troup Street, reading our homework.

When Grace charged into the classroom after a homework session, we read the bad news in her stormy countenance. Bang on the desk went the stack of essays, and Grace launched. She was unstinting in her criticism and parsimonious with her praise. Snatching student example after example from the stack, and reading aloud, she explicated the offenses in each sentence and paragraph.

Back our essays came as do-overs, the margins shockingly

red with remarks and demands. We would be told to write the essays again. And this pattern went on until, one by one, each student produced a product that was acceptable.

My frustration was almost palpable. My ego rebelled at this treatment and at Grace's demands to avoid clichés, to use the active voice, to be specific, to simplify, simplify, simplify. But then—when an essay was deemed acceptable—Grace's approval was the greatest reward. Her arthritic fingers reached to select an essay from the stack. Her face relaxed into pleasure. Mine! She'd chosen mine. Approvingly, even radiantly, she'd read the exposition.

It was Grace Durrin who first wagged "the little book" in the air and ordered us to the campus bookstore to buy copies. The MacMillan Company had published *The Elements of Style* just a year earlier, and I trundled off obediently to buy my copy. I still have it. Dog-eared now, its orange cover faded, the binding glue fragile, my first copy—the Eleventh Printing, 1960—is the one I reach for although there are several later revisions in our house.

As the campus trees started to leaf out that spring and final exams were threatening, the stacks of books Grace carried to class grew heavier. She was retiring at the end of the semester and with plans, perhaps, to move from Troup Street, she was reducing her library. What we now call down-sizing. Entering the classroom those last weeks, she'd slam the books on her desk and urge us to take whatever we wished.

Reverently, I took my turn "shopping" and selected several volumes. One of them—*The Reading of Poetry*—is on my desk as I write this. Published by The Riverside Press in 1939, it is rich with example—an amazing compendium of poetry mechanics. The book is heavily underlined, and I see the still-familiar evidence of Grace's hasty pen at work, impatiently and eagerly marking passages and applauding phrases with the vigor she applied to grading student papers. But the element of the book I most treasure is written on the flyleaf in her familiar hand:

Grace Durrin
116 Troup Street
Bowling Green, Ohio

P.S. As I reread this expository essay I can't help but feel Grace's frowning disapproval. And finishing that sentence, the phrase "I can't help but feel" sent me to the little book to be scolded by Strunk and White. Sure enough, I can't help feeling would be the preferred construction. Ever the humble student.

OLD DAME DANCING

TRANSFORMATIONS

An old film of *Inside the Actor's Studio* turned up in a television search last night and—luck of all lucks—Robin Williams was James Lipton's guest. Mr. Doyle and I settled back for two hours of laughter. He was a genius, Robin Williams, and it was the genius of James Lipton to relax, slacken the line and let it play out until Williams had gone as far out as he wished. Lipton didn't reel him in; he simply waited calmly, then asked the next question.

Williams did it all. He recreated the dances from Aladdin ("Bob Fosse, Bob Fosse. Twyla Tharp, Twyla Tharp"). He borrowed a pink scarf from a young woman in the audience and in rapid succession, transformed himself from a Muslim to a woman, a rabbi, then an iron chef. He chattered animatedly, and convincingly, in French, Yiddish, and the broad Scots without speaking an actual word of any language. Each character simply obeyed some internal summons and bloomed, as an entirely recognizable character. Each transformation was seamless.

Now, Robin Williams is an extraordinarily gifted talent, but I recognized—on a much-reduced scale, of course—the similar challenge presented to a ghostwriter. The writer must not only listen to the subject, the writer must become that individual if the written piece is to be authentic. A good ear is invaluable, but there is something else—some ineffable quality possessed of the subject, that the writer must absorb, or process, and then translate.

One of my most rewarding and pleasurable ghostwriting tasks was provided by a wonderful friend who wanted a memoir for his children and grandchildren. He was well known in the community and was much beloved, famous for his dry New England humor and a natural storyteller.

We began our work.

I explained that I would record our sessions and after each, would write up the story and submit it to him for comment. I produced the initial draft and he was dismayed. He didn't like the way he sounded.

"I sound like a ridge runner," he said.

I wasn't certain what a ridge runner was, but I had an idea what he meant. The writing wasn't fancy enough.

I explained my conviction that this was *his* story—a first-person memoir that he was supposed to have written—and therefore, the writing had to be in his voice. Had to be.

"Your kids want you to tell the story," I asserted. "I could write it in my style—in any style—but it wouldn't sound like you."

He reluctantly agreed with this logic, and we pressed on. But he remained unconvinced, though he was too polite to press me too hard.

The memoir was published and his kids loved it. So did his friends and the vast number of relatives in his extended family. They couldn't get over it.

"I could hear Gordon on every page," they said.

"It sounded just as if he was talking to me."

So, I won that one. Pardon me if I gloat just a bit about it. I'm no Robin Williams (who is?) but my message is this: a writer has to have a touch of what Williams had—an uncanny facility for transforming himself or herself into the character under construction. Whether it is a paying client or a fictional person in a novel, that character has to be authentic. Authentic, even if he's nattering away in language that is meant to sound something like Farsi.

MOVE OVER, MR. WEBSTER

"Do you know what ratchet means?"

"Certainly," I told Mr. Doyle with confidence. "It's a mechanical device that permits continuous linear or rotary motion in only one direction while preventing motion in the opposite direction."

Mr. Doyle regarded me calmly.

"You're sure about that?"

"Well...yes," I said. "Look it up."

"Look it up where?" he queried. There was a devil's advocate quirk to his brow.

"Where you'd look anything up." I was growing annoyed. "Merriam-Webster's Dictionary. New World Dictionary. Google it, for heaven's sake."

"How about The Urban Dictionary?" he said. "If you looked there you would find that ratchet is a diva, most generally from a city, who thinks she is every man's eye candy."

He looked smug.

"Urban Dictionary? Well, nobody would take that seriously, would they?"

"Oh, quite the contrary. There's a new, modern language out there. Best to be informed."

He winked.

Well, I certainly don't want to be linguistically left in the dust. Moreover, I feel I owe it to my geriatric readers to keep up-to-date on changing mores and folkways, including the English language, which I love and respect, so I ankled it trippingly to Google Chrome to find out more.

Urban Dictionary was originally intended to catalog slang and cultural phrases not found in ordinary dictionaries. Blackballed from them, I assumed. The wretched idea got out of control very quickly, with all manner of people submitting their favorites—excuse me, favs—to the online site. When I consulted Wikipedia (one of my go-to favs for quick explanations), I learned that Urban Dictionary contains more than seven million definitions with 2,000 new entries being added every day. Volunteer editors and site visitors review these submissions, which come zooming in through Facebook and gmail accounts, and the words and phrases that pass muster, get boosted up to the free site.

Well, you get what you pay for.

I rifled the virtual pages in the dictionary and determined that most of the entries are too vulgar to repeat in a respectable essay written by an old dame, but I did find out that Urban Dictionary is routinely consulted by certain professionals in order to determine whether bounds are being exceeded or vulgarities are being innocently employed. The Department of Motor Vehicles, for instance, not wishing to grant vanity plates with secret, lewd meanings, regularly goes online to help make determinations. Trial attorneys, some of whom have clients who communicate almost exclusively in street talk, often consult Urban Dictionary to be clear about what those clients are saying.

So maybe Urban Dictionary is a good idea. But there is an evil genius somewhere in charge of bollixing things up.

So here's what happened when someone got the bright

idea to feed the contents of the dictionary into Watson, the artificially intelligent computer system that IBM designed for *Jeopardy*. It seemed reasonable. After all, Watson was designed to answer questions that are asked in natural language. But Watson couldn't distinguish between the polite and the profane, or between acceptable language and cuss words. First thing you know, Urban Dictionary's words got all scrambled up with Watson's resident vocabulary—which was quite considerable—and Urban Dictionary completely polluted the computer's vocabulary. A researcher discovered the problem when he asked Watson a question and the computer answered, "Bullshit." According to Atlantic Magazine, it took a 35-person team, working hard and fast, to develop a filter to curb Watson's swearing and to purge The Urban Dictionary from its memory.

But let's get back to the word that started this whole thing—ratchet. "Ratchet," and here I quote exactly from Urban Dictionary, "is a diva, mostly from urban cities and ghettos, that has reason to believe she is every mans eye candy. Unfortunately, she's wrong."

Some of the grammar in this definition is incorrect. There's a punctuation error too. And aren't all cities urban?

Perhaps Urban Dictionary needs its own grammar textbook. And a style sheet.

OLD DAME DANCING

AN EVENING WITH JOAN PARKER

I saw Robert B. Parker once. He was giving a lecture in Andover, Massachusetts, the movie *Spenser for Hire* had just moved into production, and I was excited to be in the audience. Years later, I met Bob's wife—his widow by that time—and Joan Parker was something. By the end of the evening, I could understand why Spenser, Parker's detective, was endlessly and enduringly smitten with Susan Silverman, Joan's alter ego.

The Flint Memorial Library had invited Joan Parker to talk about her late husband in an interview-format event, and I was asked to be an interviewer. I did some homework.

This is what I knew: I knew the Parkers had lived for many years in our next-door town. Then they'd moved to Cambridge, and after a short estrangement, had worked out an unusual living arrangement in a large Victorian house on Linnean Street where Bob occupied one floor and Joan, with a separate entrance, lived upstairs. Bob dedicated every Spenser book—and he was a prolific writer—to Joan. The Parkers share writing credits on two books: *Three Weeks in Spring* (Houghton Mifflin, 1978) recounts their experience with Joan's breast cancer, and a coffee table book, *A Year At The Races* (Viking Penguin, 1990), details a period when the Parkers owned a share in a thoroughbred called Summer Squall. They shared the books' credits, but the writing was Bob's. Starting with *The Godwulf Manuscript*, I had read my way through almost every book Parker had published.

This is what I found out: That Joan Hall Parker met Bob as a child in Pittsfield and the two met again as students at Colby. She was a professor of early childhood growth and development at Endicott College and later, was director of curriculum for public schools in northeastern Massachusetts. She could, according to her son Dan, swear "like no other. She was a just a fearless woman with a great heart." Returning from yoga one June morning in 2010, she found her husband in his study, dead of a heart attack.

This is what I was unprepared for: Joan Parker was a stunning woman in fitted leather pants and boots, a knuckle-dusting ring and huge sunglasses pushed up on her brown pageboy and worn, I assumed, since it was nighttime, as a fashion accessory. Trim and fit, at once elegant and athletic looking, she was three months shy of her eightieth birthday, and she could have easily passed for fifty. Her late husband, at that moment, might have said she was like a jar in Tennessee. She made the slovenly wilderness surround that hill.

Joan Parker had a low-pitched, drawling voice and the droll timing of the master wit. She was also an excellent interview. You could ask her a question or feed her a line and what you got back was no unsatisfactory one-word response; you got a thoughtfully developed, witty answer that, if you were just patient, she would spin out into story. She may not have been a writer, but she was a storyteller, pure and natural.

Joan Parker seemed willing to field any question—personal or professional. So of course I asked about her alter ego Susan Silverman, Spenser's longtime love interest (Spenser calls her his honey). Joan made a wry face, and I offered to shift subjects, when she obligingly opened up about her relationship with Susan.

From the March, 2013 interview:

On Susan Silverman:

Joan Parker: Susan and I had a love-hate relationship, particularly in later years. I said to Bob, she's so *annoying* in her adulatory demeanor.

Robert B. Parker: You see—you don't get it. Susan is my idealization of you.

Joan Parker: Oh, I get that. She's still annoying.

Robert B. Parker had been gone nearly three years at the time of the Flint interview, and his enormously popular novels were being continued by anointed writers. Ace Atkins had won the Spenser series and Michael Brandman (less successfully) was doing Jesse Stone. Joan exercised strong influence in the appointments of Parker's successors, and she was particularly pleased with Atkins. She admitted that his name—Ace (her husband's nickname)—had immediately predisposed her to the young writer from New Orleans. But the search for a Sunny Randall author was still ongoing.

"If I could write," she lamented, "if I could only write, I would be perfect to do Sunny Randall. However, I have no talent when it comes to writing other than term papery things. But I do hear it [the voice] and I do recognize it."

On voice:

"There are readers who care about character. Other readers just want storyline. Or humor. Others, like myself, are looking for the voice. They just want to hear that voice."

I asked her to comment on Atkins's success in continuing Spenser's voice.

"He (Parker) had a PhD in English lit—American lit—and he would slip literary references in. I think no one else could do that, nor could most people—including myself—know the reference. And I'd say what the hell is that? And he'd say where it came from and he would begin to quote."

Interviewer: "Can Ace (Atkins) do that?"

Joan Parker: "No. And I don't think he needs to."

Joan Parker had put an unerring finger on one of the Parker hallmarks that is, in my opinion, vastly underappreciated—his use of literary allusion and reference. Finding and identifying them is a favorite game of mine. Sometimes the reference is no more than a fragment—a sideswipe—with no quotation marks to alert the reader to the allusion. It was Parker tipping a wink to fellow English majors perhaps but more likely simply amusing himself.

Somewhere in the vaults of *youtube*, the Flint Library's *An Evening with Joan Parker* is alive and well and rolling still. The filming was semi-professional, the room was poorly lighted and—as there invariably is—there was a cougher in the audience. But the video has merit anyhow. And there again, in an hour interview, Joan Parker, elegant and affable, speaks with inimitable style about her late husband Robert B. Parker, who once wrote: *I was there with the women who manage my life: Helen Brann, who is my literary agent; Flora Roberts, who is my dramatic rights agent; and Joan Parker who is the source of music from a distant hill.*

That evening, perhaps I heard a snatch of music from that distant hill, for I was deeply affected by the interview with Joan Parker. So I was incredulous, just a few weeks later, on that morning in June, 2013, to read in *The Boston Globe* that Joan Parker had died of lung cancer. She sent me a note shortly after our interview, and I believe she was sincere when she wrote "I hope we meet again."

Perhaps we will.

∼

OLD DAME DANCING

EVERYTHING IS MEMOIR

I am reading Nora Ephron's *Heartburn*. Actually, I am re-reading it. Well, if you want the whole truth, I am re-re-re-reading it. *Heartburn* is one of my go-to books when I run out of reading material or when every other book around the place sours or when I simply want to immerse myself in one of the best writing voices around.

Heartburn is a novel but it is also a memoir. So it's a novelized memoir? A memoirized novel? Well, whichever, it follows pretty closely the events around Ephron's second divorce—a divorce that came about when she was seven months pregnant with her second child. Husband Number Two, the man she was divorcing, was Carl Bernstein of Bernstein-and-Woodward fame and a well-known Washington columnist, political commentator and skirt-chaser. And in my opinion a rat. I have stronger opinions about Mr. Bernstein as well, but I'm trying to take the high road here, so you'll have to settle for rat.

Ephron sliced this dramatic section out of her life and molded it into a lucrative novel, bearing out what I repeatedly tell my memoir students—that they don't have to write their whole life stories from birth and onward. If they *did* write their whole stories from birth forward, they would be writing an autobiography. Of course, an autobiography is a memoir too, but a memoir isn't necessarily an autobiography. Autobiography is the story of a life; memoir is a story *from* a life, and the writer is free to lift any section from that life and simply write about that. And so Nora Ephron chose to write about her divorce from Carl Bernstein, whom she called Mark Feldman, but everyone knew it was Carl Bernstein.

Mark Feldman is involved with Thelma Rice, the wife of the Undersecretary to the Middle East, Jonathan Rice, but everyone knew that Jonathan Rice was really meant to be Peter Jay, the British ambassador and that Thelma Rice was a thinly disguised Margaret Jay.

It sounds terribly sad, I know, but Ephron manages to be witty as well as sad, and she's candid too and she even manages to throw in some recipes including one for a New York-style cheesecake that always makes me wonder if there's any Philadelphia cream cheese in the house. And then there is that voice. When it comes to dialog, Nora Ephron has perfect pitch.

So what about this issue of memoirized novel? Ephron certainly isn't the first to step into the genre. I think Harper Lee does it in *To Kill A Mockingbird*. And don't tell me that Mary McCarthy didn't lift most of *The Group* straight out of her Vassar dorm room.

Besides *Heartburn*, I've also been reading Mary Karr's text *The Art of Memoir*. In fact, it was *The Art of Memoir* that sent me scurrying to *Heartburn*. Karr was getting a little strident, I thought. A little harsh. She kept plucking the harp string about veracity in memoir. Ya gotta tell the truth and the whole truth and nothing but. She is vehemently opposed to fictionalized memoir, but I have no idea what she'd say about memoirized fiction. Maybe she'd give it a break as long as the author wasn't trying to pass it off as memoir. Mary Karr has very strong opinions about memoir. I bought her book based on a review I read and because the review led me to believe she had a sense of humor. But no. Now I don't think she does.

Nora Ephron now—*she* has a sense of humor. A great sense of humor.

If there's one thing I have to say about memoir, it's that there are no rules. It's your story and you can write any way you damn please. You can write in poetry, you can write it in bulleted copy, you can write it *backwards*, if you want. You can change names if you feel like it and you can either explain that you are changing them, or you can go right ahead and turn Carl Bernstein into Mark Feldman and let everyone else figure it out. You can follow Mary Karr's imperative to write truth, the whole truth and nothing but and produce a memoir that broadcasts every seedy detail of a sexually abused girl growing up in Texas. Or you can write your memoir and call it a novel.

Because *everything* is memoir. Everything. On some level, we're all writing out of our own experience. Even the guy writing sci-fi is applying his own observation and emotions and yes, even his experience, to the extreme fantasy he is creating.

Every thing I've ever written—including technical advertising copy—has risen out of my experience and is, in some way—sometimes a remote way—memoir. You can only write what you know.

OLD DAME DANCING

We grow neither better nor worse as we grow older, but more like outselves.

                Mary Lamberton Beecher

LOOKING BACKWARD

OLD DAME DANCING

OLD DAME DANCING

JUMPING ROPE

The beefy man on *youtube* is lecturing on the cardiovascular benefits of jumping rope. High tech fitness machines make an expensive backdrop as he instructs novices to keep the shoulders low and to permit the wrists to do the turning. Wrists only! The rope, he explains, must be carefully sized to fit the jumper; the ideal rope has ball bearings and is made of durable vinyl. Such a rope can be purchased for fifteen or twenty dollars.

He demonstrates proper jumping techniques, bouncing for a while on the balls of his feet, then announces a more advanced jump—three bounces on one foot then three hops on the other foot. Wow! Then, finally—but only for the well advanced he cautions—skipping!

I am amused.

On the playground of the elementary school where I did most of my rope jumping, we were ignorant of all these things the beefy man knows. We'd never heard the word cardiovascular. Skipping (the advanced technique) was simply the way we traveled back and forth between school and home. Our ropes weren't vinyl and ball bearings were only for our roller skates. Our ropes were lengths of clothesline begged from our mothers. They were white in the early spring and gray by the time the blossoms opened on the trees.

Length is important—the beefy man had that right. Of what use is a short rope? A decent rope must be long enough for several girls to jump at once. When we wanted to jump solo, we simply wound the excess rope around and around our hands until it was short enough for a little girl to skip over it daintily.

But solo jumping is only for emergencies. The fun is in community.

Two girls volunteer as turners. They stand ten to twelve feet apart and begin turning. The rope starts its familiar springtime slap-slap-slap-song against the pavement. The other girls form a queue and begin to feel the rhythm. Then Kathy jumps into the turning rope and the chant begins.

Down in the meadow where the green grass grows/There sat Kathy as sweet as a rose/ Along came JACK and kissed her on the nose/How many kisses did she get?

The rope turns faster—it's whirling now—and Kathy's jumping shifts from an easy double-bounce to an intense jump-jump-jump and the fascinated chanters count.

"1-2-3-4-5-6-..."

How many kisses? When will the rope trip her allowing Jack to stop his amorous advances?

But Kathy is skilled. When she tires, she simply slips the cage of the turning rope and arrives laughing and breathless on the other side.

Jump rope rhymes. We have our favorites.

Mabel, Mabel/Set the table/ Don't forget the red hot pepper!

And the rope turns madly as the jumper jumps for her life.

Miss Mary Mack-Mack-Mack/All dressed in black-black-black/ With silver buttons-buttons-buttons/All down her back-back-back/ She asked her mother-mother-mother/For fifty cents-cents-cents/ To see the elephants-elephants-elephants/Jump the fence-fence-

fence...

The best ones are the motion chants—the rhymes that require the girls to act out the movement called for in the chant.

Charlie Chaplin went to France/To teach the elephants the hula-hula dance/ (hip swivel)/ *Heel, toe, around we go* (360 degree turn in the air and repeat)/*Heel, toe, around we go/ Salute to the captain, curtsey to the queen (*salute and curtsy)/*And touch the bottom of the submarine!* (Slap the ground and jump back up again before the rope completes the full arc).

Teddy bear, teddy bear, turn around/Teddy bear, teddy bear, touch the ground/Teddy bear, teddy bear, go upstairs/Teddy bear, teddy bear say your prayers/Teddy bear, teddy bear, turn off the light/Teddy bear, teddy bear, say goodnight.

Two new turners take over and a new pair jumps together for a while, face to face. A doubles chant begins.

All in together, girls/Never mind the weather girls...

Now the line of girls runs through the spinning rope in a drill team style.

"Double-Dutch" someone orders and two ropes spin—one clockwise, the other counter—and still the drill keeps running. Now three girls risk jumping in trio; they bounce in rhythm to the chants until the bell ending recess rings across the playground.

Long gray lengths of clothesline are hastily gathered into loose coils and the girls run for the school door. Cheeks are rosy; hair is windblown. Breathing hard and cardiovascularly fit, we open our arithmetic books.

Oh big, beefy man in your expensive sneakers, turning your perfectly-sized ball-bearing rope, what rhymes do you know?

OLD DAME DANCING

THE TASTE OF PASTE

Every September, each student in my elementary school classroom was furnished with a few standard supplies: two wooden pencils, a box of fat crayons, a jar of school paste with a blue-and-white checkerboard label, an artgum eraser, and a tablet of yellow paper, Goldenrod brand. There was an intended use for each of these items. We found others.

    Wooden pencils were for biting. There was no malicious intent here, just the mildly pleasant sensation of molars penetrating painted wood. While the teacher was talking or while you were supposed to be adding up a page of sums, you could simultaneously occupy yourself with chomping. Many pencils were so badly bitten that you were unable to tell whether the paint had been red, yellow or blue. Some kids bit the ferrules too—those metal things that hold the erasers on the pencils—but the idea of metal fillings contacting the metal ferrules made me shutter, so my ferrules were always intact, even when the erasers were worn flat,

    Crayon boxes were ordered out for art class and whenever the National Safely Council supplied posters to color. Each poster had a cautionary message: "Stop-Look-and-Listen" "Only Cross At Corners" "Look Both Ways". But when we weren't coloring safety posters or drawing turkeys for Thanksgiving, I liked to smell the crayons. Like a connoisseur of fine cigars, I'd draw each crayon back and forth below my nose and inhale. The orange crayon smelled different from all the rest. I don't know why, it just did. I could recognize that crayon blindfolded.

Paste. Everybody sampled it. You'd wipe out a dab on a finger and lick it. But paste is like a drug. One taste leads to another, then to addiction. One day Tommy Parks, who sat in front of me, ate half a jar. Then, of course, when we had some pasting project—something like cutting autumn leaves out of construction paper and sticking it onto a regular piece of paper or making paper chains—Tommy had to borrow paste from me.

Artgum erasers—well of *course* we ate them. If they didn't want us to eat them, they would have called them something else, dontcha think? They'd have called them art *eraser* or *big, white eraser*. But *gum*! Gum was for chewing—you couldn't fool us about that! Ordinarily, we weren't allowed to chew gum in school, which was another thing about these erasers. Chewing them was sort of flaunting the rules. This is the protocol for artgum eraser consumption: crumble bits off the eraser, working from the corners, roll the bits into balls, then nibble them. You had to be careful rolling though. The shreds of eraser tended to get quite dirty while rolling back and forth on your desk, and black shreds of artgum weren't as appealing as that big, soapy white chunk you started with.

The company that manufactured Goldenrod elementary school wide-ruled writing tablets must have held a profitable monopoly on school business. I cannot imagine how many tablets of that rough, yellow paper I personally covered with penmanship practice letters and attempts to solve arithmetic problems. It was useful. It was cheap. And it was excellent for spitballs. Here is how to manufacture a spitball. Tear off a bit of tablet paper. As the sheets on a tablet decrease, jagged bits of paper remain at the glued binding where sheets have torn off raggedly. These are the bits you want for spitballs; they are the perfect size. Put the paper in your mouth and chew it into a firm ball. Seal ball with your saliva. Work the spitball to the center of your pursed lips, take aim and use your tongue to propel the spitball at a fellow student. Resume facing the front of the classroom and try to look innocent.

Then stare at the school clock over the doorway and count the probable number of ticks this clock will make until you're dismissed for lunch.

OLD DAME DANCING

THE WAY WE WORE

I base my fashion sense on what doesn't itch.
Gilda Radner

When did I stop wearing high-heeled shoes? I remember walking—well, limping—into my office one morning, it must have been around 1993, slipping off my fashionable pump and kicking the damn thing clear across the office. It hit the fax machine, which should give you an even clearer idea of the year or at the very least, of the decade. Like Deedle-deedle dumpling, my son John, I limped across the office, picked up the offending shoe, and limped to the phone to finally make an appointment with a podiatrist to have an ingrown toenail removed. That toenail was the direct result of wearing pointy-toed, pinchy-toed, fashionable high-heeled shoes. Post toenail removal I started shopping for shoes that had plenty of room in the toe.

That was how my mother judged style. Plenty of room in toe. She repeated the mantra about nine times whenever she took me shoe shopping. I was made to stand with all my weight on one foot while my mother and the shoe salesman took turns feeling my feet and pressing with their thumbs to ascertain the amount of room I had. Then they'd factor in some extra "room to grow."

Do you remember those machines in shoe stores? Shoe-fitting fluoroscopes they were called. Or pedoscopes. You, the fit-ee, (i.e. the child) inserted your feet in the box; then you looked down through a porthole at your bones in a watery green sea and at the silhouette of the shoe under consideration. On the other side of the fluoroscope, the fit-ers—your mother and the salesman—were provided with viewing portholes too, and there was much peering and discussing as they tried to determine the best possible fit for your feet.

Then atom bomb tests started blowing up New Mexico and those pedoscopes disappeared—a health hazard, it turned out. Suddenly, radiation poisoning and the Cold War were the headlines, and schoolchildren learned to crawl beneath their desks and shield their heads with their crossed arms so as to protect themselves effectively during the atomic blast that would release a radiation poison even stronger than a fluoroscope's. Anyhow, that was the end of pedoscopes, and my mother and the salesmen went back to simply feeling my feet to ensure toe room and plenty of it.

High-heeled pumps never had "plenty of room in the toe". In fact, they constricted the toes leading to bunions, and the high heels pitched you forward, contributing to poor posture and later back problems, but they made your legs look terrific. My mother's friend Marge used to speak on behalf of the high heeled shoe, explaining that they did glamorous things for your legs. The higher the heel, the better, according to Marge.

My mother snorted at that, but I was an acolyte. Still, my shoes came off my feet before I put down my keys when I walked into my house. My feet froze in those shoes too. And finally there came a point where comfort trumped my desire for glamorous legs. I started buying sensible shoes. I shopped for warmth and practicality. Nothing toeless. No slingbacks.

And I wanted plenty of room in the toes.

You don't have a choice with labels though. You can't exactly shop for tagless clothing. Tags—those labels that clothing manufacturers sew inside garments. Sometimes they're used sewn at the back of the neckband where they itch, scratch, and generally drive you nuts. And if you try trimming one, the stub, which you can never fully remove, scratches even more. A lot of consumers must have complained and the manufacturers moved the tags to the side seams. They didn't discontinue them, they just sneaked them into a less public part of the garment. What? Weren't we supposed to notice? There I am, driving my car and wondering what is that annoying itchy-scratchy thing near my waist. Is it a bug of some kind? An insect? But, gosh, I can't pull over here in all this traffic to check. And then you finally get home and pull out your shirttail and find out it's a tag.

So you rip it out. You don't cut it because that leaves a stub, remember, and that's almost worse than the whole label. But while you're ripping, you also rip out the threads that secure the seam, so now you've traded the annoyance of a scratchy label for a hole in a seam.

And speaking of booby-trapped clothing, how about those little T-shaped plastic strings that hold labels onto a garment? How d'you like those? You have to get the scissors to cut the plastic (because you can't rip plastic and first you have to find the scissors). Then, when you cut, bits of plastic fly in any direction and you have to get down on your knees and feel around on the floor to get the plastic bits that you can't see because they're practically transparent. Sometimes the T part becomes embedded in the sewn hem of the garment. The best you can do is trim the end as close to the hem as possible, then try to live with the top of the T inside your clothes and the sharp splinter of its stub. This is like living with a thorn under your skin.

I wonder if Gilda Radner ever wore a crinoline petticoat. She must have. I've worn garter belts, merry widows, strapless bras, even a hoop skirt once, but the crinoline petticoat takes the trophy for itchiness. In the fab fifties, in an attempt to keep full skirts from hanging like old dustcloths from our hips, we high school girls propped up our skirts with crinoline petticoats. Layers of them. A single crinoline, even with its three tiers of net, wouldn't manage the job. I generally wore three although some girls wore as many as five.

Crinolines went limp eventually and to stiffen them up, we soaked them in sugar water then line-dried them. Sitting in classrooms all day on layers of sugar-stiffened net was more than itchy—it was stupid. What we needed then was Gilda Radner or some straight-talking, no-nonsense, tell-it-like-it-is person to stand up and say, Listen! This is crazy. Whoopi Goldberg, she could have done it. She wouldn't have stood for it. Where was Whoopi in 1957?

~

OLD DAME DANCING

THE SOUNDS OF SERVICE

Around the dawn of the Millennium I began hearing that we were entering a service economy. I could hardly believe this. Here I am, standing around in countless stores waiting in vain to be assisted by indifferent clerks. Repairmen I call promise to show up, only to be kidnapped by aliens, apparently, for they rarely appear. The promised estimate for tree trimming never comes. The stump that was to be ground out on Thursday is still intact seventeen Thursdays later. And I've logged I-don't-know-how-many hours on the phone, listening carefully because options have changed, and while my call is important and they are eager to serve me, they aren't eager enough, or else I'm not important enough, for anyone to *pick up the damn phone and speak to me!* And when I am finally connected, it is to someone in Delhi who is very earnest but whose first language isn't English. Ha! They don't know what a service economy is, these people announcing the new millennium.

    I know what a service economy is like. I grew up in one. Flashback to the 1940s and the street where I grew up. The neighborhood virtually throbbed with service.

    Milkmen hurried up driveways with quarts of fresh milk rattling in wire cages. Tin boxes waited beside back doors to receive the bottles, but we were lucky to have a milk chute—a sort of Automat arrangement of cunning, miniature doors—one inside and one outside that the milkman used to remove the washed empties and restock the fresh delivery.

Loyalties to various dairies were intense. We were Moss Farm Dairy folks. So were the Hodges, across the street. But the Roses and the Bachmans bought Meyer's Milk (which Betsy Hodges and I felt was not quite as delicious and nutritious as Moss.) Milkmen in colorful little vans with painted pictures of bucolic scenes and placid cows churtled up and down the streets.

Bakery vans featured little bells in the floor that the deliveryman tapped with his foot to announce the arrival of fresh breads and cupcakes. Spang's Red Wagon was the bakery we favored, and my mother placed a red cardboard "S" in the front window to let the Spang's man know we wanted oatmeal bread that day.

We also had an egg man. His name was Mr. Draper, and he arrived in our kitchen every other Friday morning at breakfast-time, entering without knocking and talking like a phonograph record playing at the wrong speed. Mr. Draper talked faster than any human I'd ever heard. He sounded like an auctioneer. He and my father conversed over the eggs. My father's were fried on a plate next to the bacon and toast, and Mr. Draper's were in neat rows in gray cardboard boxes. I was proud of my father, and impressed that he could understand what Mr. Draper was saying. I was in awe of Mr. Draper and a little frightened of him, but not as frightened as my friend Betsy across the street, who had flame red hair that Mr. Draper liked to tease her about.

Fuller Brush men and encyclopedia salesman, always correctly dressed in suits and neckties, respectfully rang doorbells and were invited inside by housewives to sit in living rooms and display the amazing wares in their open suitcases.

And the Fuller Brush man always left a gift for his hostess.

Men whistled. The postman, carrying the huge leather bag of U.S. Mail, whistled his way up one side of the street and down the other. Grocery deliverymen with stubby yellow pencils behind one ear, whistled up driveways with cartons of groceries. Men sawing wood and painting shingles whistled in sync with their tasks. When did men stop whistling? Why do we no longer hear those cheerful tunes of industry?

And there were the garbage men. In the 'forties, they'd harvest metal pails from containers set in the ground in each backyard, heft the odiferous vessels onto their shoulders and make for the street to shake the contents into the open beds of foul-smelling trucks.

Finally, there were the department store delivery vans. The ladies of Cleveland Heights shopped downtown at the big department stores on Euclid Avenue, leaving purchases in their wakes for fleets of store vans to deliver. The screech of van brakes was a daily sound in the neighborhood, and the deliveryman was swinging down, bellowing the name of his store, almost before the brakes set.

"Hall-llees! "Hig-bees!" "Ma-ay Com-pan-y!"

Each name had a rhythm and pitch that we children quickly learned. Children of the 'forties played outside year round in all but the most violent rain and snowstorms. When, half-frozen, we implored our mothers to open the front doors, we'd mimic the voices of the department store deliverymen.

"Hall-llees!" we'd howl, standing on cold porches, shifting from foot to foot on numb feet, and adding our small voices to the everyday sounds on our suburban street—the sounds of service. Real service.

∼

MAGGIE SEWS A DRESS

Now I will never know why my mother decided to make a dress for me. It's far too late to ask her. Goodness knows, she'd never taken such a notion before. In fact, except for a bagful of socks that she was always threatening to darn, I'd never seen Maggie sew. But sock darning was a thing Maggie thought she *should* do, and to that end, she stuffed every worn-out sock into a red cotton bag with yellow ball fringe, which gave the bag a sort of frivolous, Mexican effect. Every once in a while she brought this bag out and made a show of darning. This was always in the company of her friend Aurabelle, who also kept a darning bag, but after piercing a few socks with darning needles and creating some great lumps that would raise blisters on the heels of their families, Maggie and Aurabelle usually gave up and just drank tea.

I wish I *did* know what inspired Maggie, or drove her, to offer to make me a dress. The thing was, I didn't need a new dress. If I'd needed one, Aunt Mary would have whipped up a perfect one in short order. Aunt Mary was in charge of my wardrobe, and she was a gifted and exacting seamstress. Up until the moment of her abrupt dress-making decision, my mother had been relieved and pleased that her sister was the willing wardrobe mistress.

Another thing that I wonder is why I went along with Maggie's plan. I was fifteen and certainly had no illusion that my mother could sew. And I should have been suspicious about why she suddenly wanted to, but the first thing I knew—at least the first thing I clearly remember now—is plowing in Maggie's wake through the yard goods department of Halle Bros. in search of fabric and a pattern.

But in the yard goods department—of all places—we ran into Hilda Gibbons, fresh from lunch at the Cleveland Athletic Club next door and looking, as usual, quite smart. Hilda was surprised to see us in the fabric department, and we couldn't imagine what *she* was doing there either. I think she was just passing through on her way to some other department, millinery probably or shoes. It was Kismet, though, and instead of dwelling on coincidences, Maggie confessed she was making me a dress.

Hilda instantly invited herself into the plot.

She, she told us proudly, actually *knew* how to sew, a claim that neither Maggie nor I could make. Apparently she had learned to sew at the Andrews School for Girls in Painesville, Ohio, and she would be delighted to lend her expertise to the event of making me a dress.

So gloved and hatted and heavily corseted, Hilda hitched herself onto an adjoining stool at one of the high counters where the Halle's people kept the pattern books. The three of us ripped through issues of Simplicity, McCall's and Vogue. Hilda advocated for a Vogue pattern but Maggie and I chose one from Simplicity. I, because I admired the full skirt, the boat neck, the shoulder bows and tiny, cinched waist of a pretty summer dress. Maggie, who I'm pretty sure was starting to feel a bit cowed, was probably influenced by the word Simplicity.

I selected a white cotton fabric with black polka dots. Hilda produced a packet of black trim that she said was smart, we found a zipper and we were all set.

Hilda, it transpired, was coming back to our house where she and Maggie planned sew the dress that very day. It was mid-afternoon by the time they set up the old Singer machine in the dining room, spread the fabric on the living room floor to cut the pattern and went hard at it. I was required to stand by to "try on".

So they cut and pinned and basted and sewed and tore stitches out and sewed new ones in. The side zipper proved troublesome and by the time they'd gotten it in and out of the dress three or four times, it looked sort of bent. But it went up and down mostly so they were satisfied.

The hours slipped away and a call was placed to Harold Gibbons at his office with instructions to come to our house instead of going the other way to Bay Village. Genial fellow that he was, Harold was happy to comply and to accept a drink from my father. They clinked glasses and prepared to work their way happily toward a late dinner hour in this convivial manner. They were enjoying themselves, commenting to each other about the industry and confusion going on around them. They were looking forward to a fashion show.

About eight o'clock the seamstresses had the dress together and somehow Maggie had also prepared some supper. Between them, my father and Harold had logged many years of experience with women—what with wives and daughters and secretaries and typing pools and so forth—and mellowed as they were with a few cocktails, pronounced the dress quite splendid. It didn't look too bad except for the waist. Even after all the gathering stitches had been drawn as tight as possible, the dress's waist was at least ten inches larger than mine. The polka dot dress hung like a bag.

Hilda was neither deterred nor discouraged.

"Belt it!" she declared. "They'll never know!"

No one asked who this "they" were, these people who would never know, but the next day Maggie went out and purchased a black leather belt, about five inches wide. This she hitched around me, stuffing and arranging the extra fabric under the belt and cinching it tight. I obediently tromped off the first dance of my high school career—the Howdy Doody mixer which was held outside and where everyone else was wearing Bermuda shorts and knee socks.

I've wondered since what sort of grade Hilda earned in that sewing class at the Andrews School for Girls. Not a high mark, I shouldn't think.

∼

THE BEST OF IT

He leaned against the doorjamb as he considered his *in loco parentis* week. His son and daughter-in-law had gone out of town, and Joe and Kate had apparently said, sure, sure thing—they'd come and stay with Lucy and see that the dog was fed and walked, the boiler was topped up, the rubbish hauled out and so forth. Sure, they'd be happy to see that Lucy got to her various practices and games.

"So how did it go?"

Joe looked tired. Also a little baffled. He shook his head and gazed into the middle distance.

"I don't know how they do it, the parents. I mean, she had to get to the gym right after school to practice for the game. Then there was the game itself. Then a music lesson. The next day another practice at the gym. Then when we get her to all the places she has to be and finally make it home, she's on the computer doing her homework. It never stopped. There was never a free minute."

"How old is Lucy?"

"Fourteen."

He was silent for a while. Out of the corner of my eye, I watched him.

"And texting." He continued, picking up the narrative.

"Who is she talking to? I must have asked myself that question a hundred times. What can she have to say every blessed minute? And how does she do that thing with her thumbs?"

I commiserated.

"I mean I have a phone," he said plaintively, "I have thumbs. But I'm damned if I can even type in someone's phone number on the first try. Lucy now, Lucy's thumbs behave like they've got lives of their own."

I was considering my own fourteenth year which was lived in the fabulous 'fifties—a time where I thought I was perfectly happy but probably wasn't. The television was only turned on when my sister and I had convincingly demonstrated that our homework was finished. Bedtimes were strictly observed. The telephone was very popular and my sister and I raced each for first dibs whenever it rang, but the time and competition probably limited us to two conversations each.

We had activities—music lessons, Girl Scouts, sock hops. Our parents drove us to some of those but they weren't on-call chauffeurs. We hoofed it to Mrs. Patterson's for piano and walked to a local church basement for scout meetings and got to the houses of most of our friends on shank's mare. And we could do that because our suburban streets were safe.

Good manners were valued. Men removed their hats indoors and rose to offer their seats to ladies. Ladies wore gloves. Stores were closed on Sundays, and recreation, after church and a big noontime dinner, was an afternoon drive with the whole family packed in the car. There were no seatbelts. "Going for a ride," this was called.

Life was simpler. There wasn't the pressure that the twenty-first century has produced. Boring? Probably. There was a *Father Knows Best/Our Miss Brooks* quality to it all that was genuine, not just an act on television.

I was reminded of something.

"Do you remember Walter Denton, Joe?"
The corner of his mouth creased in a smile.
"The young Richard Crenna, sure."
More silence.
"How 'bout *Mr. Peepers?*" he countered.
It was my turn to smile.
"Wally Cox. Haven't thought about him in years."

Both of us were viewing the middle distance now, each of us unreeling our private home movies. For us there had been no Ritalin to tame hyperactivity. There wasn't even hyperactivity—just a few boys in each class that 'acted up' a little. We had never heard of ADD and ADHD. We knew nothing of about peanut allergies. Childhood was about peanut butter and plenty of it. There wasn't time in the evenings after homework to communicate with more than two or three friends, and this we did by speaking into the mouthpiece of a telephone with a receiver pressed to one ear. We never texted nor skyped; we knew nothing of Facetime or Facebook. The closest thing I had to social media was an occasional copy of a magazine called *Photoplay*. I don't think I even wanted to be in twenty-four touch with everyone I knew. There wasn't cyber bullying because we hadn't yet explored cyberspace. Our schools didn't go into lock-down and our peers weren't dying of drug overdoses. There was some pressure to get into college, but there weren't nose-bleeding tuitions and usurious student loans. Men didn't wear baseball caps indoors when dining in restaurants.

No, I didn't envy young Lucy and her peers.
"We had the best of it, Joe," I told him quietly.
"Yeah," he said softly. "Yeah, we did."

> *You must find or create a world in which you can act in a sensible way.*
>
> B.F. Skinner,
> advising the old on living graciously

LOOKING FORWARD

OLD DAME DANCING

OLD DAME DANCING

ANTICIPATING THE TIPPING POINTS

Anticipating the tipping points in the aging process is a lot like sky-diving, I would think. I've never had to jump out of a plane, but I imagine if I *did* have to jump out of a plane, it would be important to jump at precisely the right moment. I wouldn't want to risk a premature ejaculation, and I wouldn't want to hesitate and have the optimal moment pass me by—the moment when it is too late to successfully jump. There are no do-overs in sky-diving. Well, my thesis here is that aging is a lot like sky-diving. You have to accurately predict the moment to yell Geronimo and tip over the edge. You don't want to jump too soon and you don't want to hang around until it's too late. There are no do-overs in this event either.

Geriatrics have a couple of probable tipping points to consider. One is when to stop driving a car. Another is when to pack your bags and bail out of the place you've been calling home.

For purposes of illustration, I'm going to cite Maggie. My mother. To her loving family, Maggie was alternately an inspiring role model and a horrible example. Since anticipating the tipping points was not one of her strong areas—she resisted them and aggressively denied them—she will appear here as an example.

First, driving. In her later years Maggie's driving was erratic. She'd always had a heavy foot and time accelerated its force. I think Maggie might have known she was driving beyond the expiration dates of her reflexes, vision and ability to make split-second decisions, but she told us that she'd die if she had to stop driving. She'd simply *die*. That's a passive aggressive contention, and this is the translation: if you make me stop driving, it will be *your* fault when I kick the bucket. Everyone will blame you. *And you'll be sorry!*

Of course, none of us wanted to tell Maggie that she had to turn in her car keys. We appealed to her physician to do the dirty work. After all, he'd been scandalized to learn she was still driving, and he swore he'd speak to her about it. He did. He said: "Your family is concerned about you and they think you should stop driving."

We all remember the day Maggie stormed home from the doctor's office. We'd all prefer *not* to remember.

Anyway, Maggie did stop driving but she frequently reminded us that she still *could* drive. Then she'd squint at us accusingly. Note: she didn't die. Not then.

Maggie missed the driving tipping point. It would have been more comfortable—and much safer—for all of us if she had simply turned in her keys after she took out the frame of the barn door for the third time, but she went on to widen the door considerably with a few more hits.

There are clues, you see. It's wise to heed them.

I hope I will be paying attention, but how can I be sure?

Maybe I could recruit a small pack of hatchet men to approach me when the signs show up. Then all I'd have to do is be gracious to the vigilantes when they come for me.

Another crucial tipping point is knowing when—or if—to move house. A strong argument can be made for "aging in place." There is a thought that seniors thrive best when they are able to continue living in their accustomed homes, and multiple studies back this up. I subscribe to this concept—up to a point. Aging-in-place is all well and good, but for some of us, there comes a time when it is unsafe and downright dangerous to live alone in the old homestead.

Maggie arrived at that point in her ninety-second year. She was frail in everything but her stubborn will. She had resolutely resisted a number of suggestions that would have bought her time in her own home; each offered an alternative to the ultimate tipping point. A church lady to keep her company several times a week was suggested. No. How about a college student to live upstairs and drive her on shopping errands and appointments? Uh-uh. And (God help us for suggesting it) wouldn't she like to move to a pleasant apartment in a senior living community? Insulted, she was furious we'd even suggest such a thing!

The opportunity to make her own decisions expired the morning Maggie had a minor TIA. She had dithered too long at the plane's open door and had missed her chance to jump.

She no longer qualified for a senior community, and she didn't adapt well to the assisted living place that followed the evaluation in rehab. She found it difficult to establish relationships for one thing. But her enforced transition was hard on her family too. We wanted to see our mother happy. And she was not.

I have to be prepared to face the same tipping points Maggie did. It is likely I'll have similar chances. I don't want to jump too soon. I don't want to turn in my keys—either the one to my car or the one to my front door while I can still safely enjoy the life I am presently enjoying. I know there will be compromises I'll have to make, but I hope I can make them while I still have the wit to do so—before others have to make those decisions for me.

OLD DAME DANCING

Recently I discovered two lists that might tip me off to the tipping points. First, in order to maintain my physical independence, (or so I read) I must be able to accomplish eight daily functions: get out of bed, use the toilet, eat, dress, bathe, groom, get out of a chair, and walk. Next, there are eight necessary activities of daily living; if I can't achieve these, then I am not safe to live on my own: shop for myself, prepare my own food, maintain my housekeeping, do my laundry, manage my medications, make phone calls, travel on my own, and handle my own finances.

Okay, so I have my tipping point lists, but will I be able to accept the necessary actions when I can no longer make a positive check mark beside each point? Will I recognize the tipping points myself or will my children or the neighbors or the folks at church have to step in with throat clearings and murmurs and sensitive phrasings? These issues—and the accompanying decisions—are surely among the most serious the aging person has to face. I think about this. And I wonder when my plane will be lifting off.

OUR OPTIONS HAVE CHANGED

Pay attention now because I am hoping our options will soon change. They certainly *need* to change, and now that some Baby Boomers are cashing Social Security checks, perhaps they *will* change. The sheer mass of the Baby Boomer population might be enough to do it. What I'm complaining about now are those recorded messages that start with: "Listen carefully because our options have recently changed."

So you obediently listen carefully to a rapid-fire recitation of the options, as you poise to press the proper number that will allow your issue to be addressed. The first problem is that my issues rarely fit neatly into one of the available pigeonholes. So I listen to the options again and take a guess. Sometimes I guess several times.

But just choosing the correct option doesn't necessarily get you out of the weeds. You might land in a decision tree where you have to keep making choices. And have you ever thought you were all set—maybe even started talking—only to have a recording tell that your wait for a representative won't be longer than eleven-and-a-half minutes? Ah, but there is music—music that's interrupted periodically so a voice can assure you that your call is important.

This is a parenthetical point, but as long as they're so big on giving options, why don't they give options for music-to-wait-by so you aren't forced to listen to rap, when you'd prefer West Coast jazz or something smooth from KD Lang?

But to get back on track now...

For folks who are genuinely geriatric, "Listen carefully..." is a rat hole. It's insulting and embarrassing and frustrating and sometimes just not feasible.

Many older folks have some hearing loss so listening carefully isn't possible. Many have slower reaction times and perhaps some compromised reasoning and so confusion sets in when the options are rattled off. By the time a shaky finger taps to the phone's keypad, Options 3 has expired and Option 5 is being offered.

As illustration, I'm inviting my mother in here again. When Maggie's Visa card came up for renewal, she needed to call an 800 number to activate the new card. This had to be done from her home phone. No excuses, no compromises accepted. Therefore, I had to drive to Maggie's home phone—a trip of two hours—in order to handle the update for her.

This annoyed Maggie, and it embarrassed her. It challenged her independence by requiring her to ask for help with a ridiculously simple transaction. I was annoyed too. Not because I had to take a day to help my mother—as it happened, we went to lunch and had a very pleasant visit—but thinking about the situation during the two-hour drive home, I began to get mad at the system.

I projected myself a few years into the future when I, like Maggie, might find a simple phone transaction beyond my power. This frightens me. Instead of dealing with a live person, I may have to deal with a telephone decision tree — frustrating even for one with all her faculties. Or I'll have to speak with someone whose first language is not English and who is struggling with American idiom while I am struggling with their heavily accented speech.

Driving, I drafted a mental message and sent it telepathically to the listen-carefully-options folks. Just you wait, I told them vindictively—someday you'll be old too. Your hearing won't be all that sharp and an options list will confuse you, so you'd better do something about it *now*. Design a better system. Think of something else. If you don't, you'll be sorry.

OLD DAME DANCING

AND NOBODY LIMPED

In the past several months I've sat in the lobbies of three upscale retirement lifestyle facilities. I was auditioning two of them for my distant (I hope very distant) future and I was in the third to visit a client who is writing a book. I observed lots of old people. Well, yeah—I *was* in a retirement facility, after all—what did I expect? Nevertheless, I decided, if this future was going to be mine, I'd better prepare. I decided to take notes. Turns out, there are a few things about myself that I'd like to correct while correction is still possible.

As I sat there, my client came trotting down a long stairway and briskly crossed the room to shake my hand.

Now I should say that this client is ninety-four, probably older than most of the residents blundering around the reception hall, many of them pushing walkers. He stood in marked contrast to them. He was trim, well dressed in excellent sports clothes. He was wearing a pullover sweater. It didn't have food stains. He stood up straight like the naval officer he had been seventy years earlier.

What set him apart?

My friend Judy was describing a reunion she'd had with eight college friends, none of whom she had seen for fifty years.

"I was nervous about going to that lunch," she said. "I

mean I wasn't even sure I would recognize these women—wasn't sure what I would find."

But Judy was pleasantly surprised. She'd had a very nice time. And her description of the reunion was typically economical. "No one was obese," she said, "and nobody limped."

Considering this, I tried to identify certain physical attributes that signal old age. I've come up with three: posture, weight, and gait.

Wait. I just thought of a fourth. Jaw. Don't let your lower jaw relax to the point your mouth hangs open. It's amazing how many seniors do this.

Memo to myself: Stand up straight. Wear clean clothes. Bathe often. Watch weight. Pull the spine up and keep the shoulders down. Keep the expression pleasant. Try to be positive. And keep the mouth closed—that's good advice at all times.

∼

OLD DAME DANCING

SORRY I MISSED THE SKATEBOARD
Or
Can The Silent Generation Find Happiness Among the Millennials?

They're called Generation Y. Born between 1981 and 2001, they're the folks who came along after Gen X's generational term expired. They have been parented by people who've consistently assured them that they are wonderful, and so it isn't surprising, given this assurance, that the character of this group is distinctly sunny. They tend to be hopeful, optimistic, self confident and basically happy. Although Gen Y's are often called The Millennials, I refer to them as The Insouciant Generation because everything they touch, from skateboards to technology, seems to come easily to them. Their mantra is "Whatever."

Me? I just made it into the Silent Generation (1925 to 1942) by the skin of my teeth. In the Silent Generation, the only examples of insouciance were Maynard G. Krebs and Alfred E. ("What me worry?") Neuman.

I can't ride a skateboard, although I'd like to. And while I'm not a total technological incompetent, having owned and operated more than a dozen personal computers and earned my living using them, I, like many of my generation, am not completely at ease with technology. Every time there's a computer crash or a software glitch, I leap to the panicked conclusion that I've blown up Pittsburgh. The DVD player baffles me and even the television remote is intimidating.

A Gen Y-er on the other hand, is automatically comfortable with all varieties of technological whizzbangs. They instinctively understand what to do; operating instructions aren't even required. Apparently their birth certificates have conferred automatic license to operate all computers, cell phones, VCRs, and they can effortlessly enable the GPS systems in their new cars. Yes, I'm pretty sure it's the birth certificates. Although it could be some new additive in their Pablum.

And skateboards. What an enviable mode of transportation. If only, I think, if only there had been skateboards when I was pre-osteopina. I watch these Millennials—even the grown ones who should probably know better—casually swerving along on these boards. Hopping off from time to time, then hopping back on as casually as I would brush a mosquito off my arm. Now I ask you? Would a member of the Silent Generation ever do that? No. Insouciance is not encoded in our DNA.

I know a Gen X-er who tried to take a flyer back to his youth and climbed on his Gen Y son's skateboard. Tore up his rotator cuff and went through a long, painful rehab. Furthermore, he had to listen to what his wife had to say. He should have left skateboarding to the Millennials.

Well, skateboards and technological competence are just two examples of the aplomb with which Millennials move in the world. Everything gets the casual touch. No big deal. No biggie. No problem. Whatever. And they're changing the world too. I mean they're in business now. They have desks and briefcases—except with a smart phone, you really don't need briefcases, do you? Or a desk in an office, as it turns out. With telecommuting, you hardly need to go into the office except to keep lunch dates.

But all that is beside the point. The actual point is: how does a member of the Silent Generation fit gracefully into this Millennial world? How can we blend? I've developed some rules and I keep trying to remember to put them in practice.

Be accepting of change. Refer often to the advice of Bob Dylan (another Silent Generation member, by the way) who observed that the times, they are a-changin' and advised you to get out of the way if you can't lend a hand.

Remember that nobody wants to hear your war stories. Resist the temptation to tell them.

Do not attempt to pass for a Millennial. In other words, don't ape Gen Y hair styles, dress styles, and the urge to get a large tattoo of an insect or an animal behind your right knee and continuing down to your ankle. You can't carry it off with insouciance, and even if you think you are managing it, you probably aren't. Stay clear of skateboards.

Never, never say "I can't." Ditto it's corollary: "I don't." (as in "I don't do email.") Even if you can't or you don't, don't admit that you don't or can't. When I was a child there was a radio program called Charming Children, and I'd sing along with a little ditty that went like this: "There are two things charming children do / They smile instead of cry / They never, never say I can't / They always say I'll try."

Whoops! I just told a war story, didn't I?

OLD DAME DANCING

ATTITUDE IS EVERYTHING

It was the day of New Year's Eve. I had negotiated the aisles of the supermarket, jammed with shoppers intent on gathering provisions for their holiday parties. I had waited my turn in an interminable checkout line and was attempting to ease my shopping cart out of the store, when the woman in front of me stopped short between the store's pair of electric doors. My carriage bumped her backside.

"Oops, sorry," I mumbled.

Then I saw that her exit was also blocked.

Outside, exiting shoppers were maneuvering their wagons into a herd, and when I was able to escape the second door, I too pressed into the crowd. I craned my neck to locate the cause of the jam.

A taxi had stopped in front of the ramp meant for shopping carts, completely blocking the only path to the parking lot. I watched the driver get out, walk around the car and open the back door for his passenger. She was an elderly woman, quite large, and wearing a long, fur coat that had that orange-y look that old fur coats get. She resembled a big, brown bear. The driver got ahold of a walker, got it open, and after quite a bit of effort, got his passenger out of the taxi and balanced on the contraption.

OLD DAME DANCING

The shoppers waited, some like me, probably fuming.

When the woman was sure she was safely upright and stable, she raised her eyes to the crowd and beamed at us. "Happy New Year everyone!" she cried merrily.

Instantly, the communal irritation evaporated. Smiles appeared. Several people returned her greeting, and we turned to each other and echoed her message with the greatest good will.

The taxi moved on. The merry woman and her bear-of-a-coat made their way into the store. The shoppers reassembled into an orderly queue, and moved down the ramp, dispersing in the parking lot. Trudging along, I marveled at the change this woman's attitude had made in my own outlook. Her simple, joyous greeting made the all difference. She didn't apologize for the delay she'd caused nor did she scuttle away in embarrassment. She simply uttered a wonderfully joyous announcement on this special day before a new year.

Attitude is everything.

~

OLD DAME DANCING

GROWING INTO OLD AGE

"She's growing old."

This observation is usually tinged with sorrow or pity as the speaker considers an individual in advancing old age. The unstated corollary is: "And isn't it a shame?"

Well, the observation might be spot-on, but right there, I'd like to consider the word growing instead of the word old. Growth, after all, is a natural thing. It's a positive thing. We do it all through our lives. Parents avidly monitor the weights of their newborn infants; each ounce gained implies movement in the right direction. Growth is progress. It's the habit of living things. *Growth* is healthy.

It follows then, that the phrase "growing old" should be an affirmation, I think. If we said aging or *getting* old or withering, we'd be suggesting degradation and implying that the aging person is heading directly for the exit sign. But growing—that's a good thing.

I used to get outgrown clothes from cousins and friends, and receiving them was an event. As each hand-me-down came out of the bag, I'd chose my favorites and eagerly try them on. But they were inevitably too big.

"You'll have to grow into this," my mother would say, and she'd hang the dress in the back of my closet—for inspiration perhaps? I'd sneak in to visit the hand-me-downs and hope I'd soon grow enough to wear them.

As a child, I played dress-up. Did you do that? Each of us had a bag stuffed with our mother's discarded clothing—the fancier, the better. My prize was a pink net bridesmaid's dress my mother wore in 1938. It wasn't a garment that translated from a fancy wedding to any other venue, so my mother donated it without sentiment. I thought it was wonderful. The other girls did too. Its net hem dragged on the sidewalk and grew grubby and torn; the embroidered silver leaves on the bodice grew tarnished. But to me it remained beautiful, and I longed to grow old enough to wear a gown like that. I could only try on my mother's and pretend. And wait.

Roses grow. So do tomatoes. Healthy infants grow into toddlers then into active children. Growing is the natural state of things. Withering is too, and I suppose you could look upon the aging process as withering, but I choose to think of it as forward progress. As growth.

I've started imaging the advanced old age that I'm heading for as a garment to grow into. I picture my last years as a beautiful robe that I will slip on someday. Cashmere. Cloud-soft. And the most delicate shade of shell-pink, the exact color of the inside of a conch shell. The robe doesn't fit me yet, but the day is coming when it will. And when the day comes, I hope to wrap myself in this robe and feel elegant and gentle and wise. The robe of old age is hanging there, waiting for me to grow enough to slip it on. And when I do, I will have entered the stage just before my final growth spurt into the unknowable beyond.

∽

*Today is only the tomorrow you
worried about yesterday.*
                    Unknown

PRESENT PERFECT

OLD DAME DANCING

OLD DAME DANCING

AN ELDERLY PLEASURE

> My business is to always feel a little like a fool
> and to speak of it
> Erica Jong

Years ago, when I was no older than thirty-two or three, I agreed to serve on a church committee dedicated to outreach. Or maybe it was inreach. Or maybe the effort was simply listed under 'good works'. But at any rate, the idea was to go out and call on church members who hadn't been seen for a while at services. Find out if anything was wrong. Invite them back into attendance. Let them know their absence had been noticed.

Sounded like a decent idea to me, so I accepted a short list of people to visit. One name on the list was Priscilla Long.

Now I should stop right here and explain a fact of small-town New England life. Shortly after I moved here, a new friend gave me a piece of good advice. "Be very careful what you say about anyone. Almost everyone in this town is related by blood or marriage to someone else."

I quickly discovered the truth of this and was grateful for the advice. But when I accepted the list of people to call on, I did not know—had no idea—that Priscilla Long's family had not only been citizens here for generations, but that the carved communion table in the sanctuary had been given by Priscilla herself in memory of her father who had been a long-time senior deacon. The irony—the very *chutzpah*—of calling on Priscilla Long to explain the church was lost on me.

Here endeth the history lesson.

Priscilla lived in a trailer park on the west side of Main Street. I located the address and knocked on her door. I stood there for several minutes, but at last the door opened and the person I took to be Priscilla Long looked out at me.

I explained who I was and what I wanted.

In the years that would follow this visit, I came to know Priscilla, although never terribly well, and I knew her to be a lady in the old-fashioned, reserved sense. She was quiet, private, and not one to waste words, but when she did speak, she was firm and clear and did not expect to be contradicted nor argued with. She was always well-dressed in the gloves-and-hat sense and every silver hair stayed where it was supposed to stay.

Okay, so I'm standing at the door of Priscilla Long's trailer, explaining my mission.

"Well," she said, "I am soaking my feet, but I suppose you can come in."

Her tone held no enthusiasm even as she held the door open. I stepped into the trailer's living room and there, indeed, was a basin of soapy water on a spread towel with the accouterments of a pedicure all around.

I sat down where she indicated, and Priscilla resumed her seat behind the basin, although she did not put her feet back in the water. We conducted the social call stiffly but as best we could under the awkward circumstances during which time I tried very hard not to look at her feet. As soon as possible, I stood to leave, and I, a complete newcomer to the shores, invited Priscilla Long to attend the church of her forebears—the church where she'd been baptized. And then I escaped feeling like a fool, and leaving her to resume her foot soaking, except the water had probably grown quite cold.

We served civilly together on several church committees, in the decades that followed, Priscilla and I, but we never became close and never referred to the circumstances of our meeting. Every time I think of it, I wince.

Now this is the point of what I've written. While I was sitting there across from Priscilla Long's foot bath, I couldn't appreciate the extreme pleasure of soaking one's feet. It seemed like such an elderly thing to do. I couldn't look into the future far enough to anticipate the day when I myself would regard foot soaking as a real closet pleasure, if an intimate one. These days I look forward to filling a basin with very hot water, adding a slug of Epsom salts, and closing the bathroom door. After ten or fifteen minutes of soaking, I dry my tootsies carefully and massage them with scented cream. Then I put on socks and for the next hour or so, enjoy the delicious sensation of warm, soft, squashy toes.

Here's the thing though. After I've closed the door and slipped my feet into their bath, Priscilla Long's ghost frequently joins me in the bathroom. (Ghosts can walk right through closed bathroom doors.) There I sit, soaking, and in she comes—the uninvited memory as fresh and embarrassing as it was forty years ago. My privacy is compromised and it serves me right.

~

OLD DAME DANCING

CONCESSIONS AT CHRISTMAS

*Christmas is coming
and we're the fat that's in the fire*
A Lion in Winter

"It's time." This had become Mr. Doyle's mantra. He had been repeating it for two or three years, but after last Christmas, he stepped up the repetitions considerably.

Time to stop standing around on freezing Christmas tree lots in December while I maundered and dithered and picked my way through the trees looking for just the right one—the one that was not too tall nor too wide, not too flat-needled nor too dried out. And, not finding the right tree in this lot, insisting we transfer our search into another forest just down the road where the process would be repeated again and again until I found the best possible tree—a small, tight Frasier fir.

It was time, he said, to stop over-paying for a Frasier fir, the BMW of Christmas trees.

Time to retire the tree saw needed to recut the frozen trunk so the tree could fit through the French door and into our family room.

Time to quit the knuckle-scraping frustration of inserting the tree into our stand—a process that always included a search for shims when the tree stand's screws proved too short (and they always proved too short) to stabilize the trunk.

Time to stop trying to remember to refill the stand's five-gallon canister every day, and time to stop worrying that an undetected hairline crack in the plastic stand would release the water and flood the room. Again.

Time to retire from the conundrum of untangling the snarls of half dozen strings of lights and to stop wondering which bulb in the string had expired, taking with it three yards of illumination.

Time to end the wrestling match of getting the dry tree out of the house on New Year's Day, with needles dropping, accompanied by a great deal of vacuuming.

Time to remember that we had to remove the tree in time for the town-wide tree collection; otherwise the tree would lie on its side beside the street like a bloated corpse, slowly turning from green to brown.

"It's time," Mr. Doyle said firmly. "This year it's time."

I acquiesced. Finally. I knew this was one more milestone in our aging process and that it was time for me to accept it.

So together we set out on our last Christmas tree hunt. Instead of heading for a frozen lot, however, we headed for an upscale garden store in Lexington and were prepared to be dazzled by the variety and magic of a forest of enchanted artificial trees. We were dazzled alright, by the sparkling array of trees. We just weren't prepared for the price of our dazzlement.

The scent of balsam engulfed us we stepped through the door, thanks to a display of miniature pine pillows and bits of incense that could be stuffed into the chimneys of tiny log cabins and burned. Literally dozens of lighted and decorated artificial tress swept us into the enchantment.

Joanne was our salesperson. She was not wearing a wool

hat and a down vest, and she wasn't blowing on reddened knuckles. This was the first time I'd met a Christmas tree salesperson whose nose wasn't running. Joanne was very knowledgable. She showed Mr. Doyle how to remove and reinsert each bulb on the pre-lit tree. She explained how the tree came in three easy pieces for storage. She phoned out to the warehouse and directed Mike to have a six-foot Flatrock fir waiting for us "down back". Then she kindly took my credit card, and I signed the receipt. In the warehouse, down back, Mike wished us a very cordial Happy Thanksgiving.

Mr. Doyle was probably right. It was time. Time on our personal continuum to make this move of convenience. So we will no longer be taking our old bones to freezing, windswept tree lots where we will stamp our feet to keep the blood flowing in our toes and get fresh sap on our gloves as we reach through branches to grasp each trunk. We won't be sweeping needles out of the car until Easter. And we will no longer be doling out horrifying amounts of cash for Frasier firs. Sure, this new artificial tree cost a pretty penny, but as I pointed out to Mr. Doyle, we can amortize the cost over the years to come. The crossover point will come in thirteen years, at which point the artificial tree will start paying for itself.

~

LIFE RAFT

> *Time that blows on the kettle's rim*
> *waits to carry us off*
> Maxine Kumin

The raft upon which we all float on the sea of life is large, but more and more frequently, more and more of the people I care about are slipping off. I understand that one day I, too, will slide over the edge into an unknowable abyss, but what that abyss may be—and what I hope is—will be some blissful state of grace. I wonder whether my slide will be graceful or whether I will be one who turns back to claw frantically at the raft's edge, unwilling to let go and go gentle into that good night.

In the meantime, I am still here on the life raft. Still witness to the release of others and a sorrowing witness to the inconsolable grief of those we call "the survivors."

Mr. Doyle and I know too well that the taste of grief is indescribable. And even when you know its sharp edges will eventually soften, grief rides you mercilessly in the meantime. The inevitability of grief moves closer with time, and I am at the age when it is a companion, close as a shadow. Grief is a sniper who picks us off one by one.

OLD DAME DANCING

Not long ago Eleanor slipped off the raft. I had known Eleanor for years, known her to be a sizey lady—tall, not fat exactly, but large-boned and on the hefty side. It is always a jolt when someone of my own vintage dies, and so I got a little shock when I opened the newspaper and the impact of Eleanor's obituary smacked me full in the face. She had died very suddenly and unexpectedly of a massive stroke. I made plans, of course, to attend the calling hours at the funeral home.

I have gotten to know—quite well in fact—the men in black suits who staff Croswell's Funeral Home, which is the establishment used by most citizens of this town. They know me by sight too, these men, and we nod cordially to one another (in fact, we are a little more familiar than I'd like to be.)

Anyhow, I signed the guestbook and inspected the pram-to-prom photographs of Eleanor's earlier days that somebody—her daughters-in-law?—had assembled. And that's another thing, those photos. Sometimes I imagine my daughter and daughter-in-law trying to find suitable pictures to memorialize me. Where will they think to look? Can they decode the weird filing system on my computer? What about those stupid pictures from the 'seventies with all the big hair that made everyone look like one of the Bay City Rollers? I'd really rather not put those photos on display. Should I destroy those now?

But getting back to Eleanor.

I made the obligatory murmurs of condolence to her family, then stepped up to the coffin to pay my last respects to Eleanor herself. How exactly are you supposed to do this? I'm never quite sure. Catholics, of course, have a system. Just drop onto the convenient kneeler, cross yourself, murmur (or appear to murmur) some holy words, cross yourself again and heave yourself to your feet or have someone help heave you. I'm not Catholic however, so I just bow my head and try to look like I'm having holy thoughts. I'm not though. I don't know why, but I can't summon any holy thoughts when my shins are against a kneeler and there's somebody I'd once known laid out before me with their hands folded across their stomachs. So I fake having holy thoughts and just try to look sad.

But getting get back to Eleanor again.

Now I had seen Eleanor just the week before in the produce section of Stop 'n Shop where we were both rummaging among the aliums. She'd been evaluating scallions and I'd been perusing leeks and she'd looked fine. She hadn't been ill. Hadn't suffered any withering or debilitating disease, so I figured she'd look ... well ... pretty much like *Eleanor* there in the casket. The individual resting against the ivory satin *resembled* Eleanor, but there was so much less of her than there had been the week before. She appeared to have diminished significantly. Her hands looked tiny—smaller than mine—and the Eleanor I had always known had large, capable hands. I pictured her reaching for those scallions. I wondered about the change all the way home.

My husband had not been at the calling hours, and I wondered aloud to him about this shrinkage.

"Something goes with death," he said. "And I think it goes instantly."

He described entering the apartment of a neighbor on Beacon Hill after hearing an alarming noise. He'd found the man in bed, still warm but quite deceased.

"It was Fred, but he looked smaller somehow. The change happened immediately. And I've come to believe that when the life force leaves, the body diminishes instantly. Deflates. And I can only conclude that the force, whatever it is—perhaps it's what we call spirit— really does fill the body with life."

I don't know, but I think it may be a comforting consideration—that when the life force leaves us, like some final exhale—it is like a great sigh of relief, much like the sigh

OLD DAME DANCING

I release every night when I slide into bed and finally put the day behind me. The spirit, released, goes onto to something greater, but it leaves behind, a vacancy and a legacy of grief for others to mourn.

∽

> *White: Was very sorry to hear about your father, and send my sympathy, which is about all I have to say, except that after you get to be thirty people you know keep dropping off all the time and it's a hell of a note.*
> *Harold Ross in a sympathy note to E.B. White*
> *quoted by Roger Angell in*
> *This Old Man*

A LONG WAY FROM THE CENTER MAYFIELD

Once we were installed uneasily in our seats, Mr. Doyle and I tried to remember the last time we'd been to the movies. We finally worked out that it had been several years earlier in a Newburyport art theater where the chairs were apparently hand-me-downs from some high school auditorium. Well. Now here we were, in a first-run theater and let me tell you, things in the movie trade have changed. Cinema Showcase is a long way from the Center Mayfield where my model of movie-going was shaped.

In purchasing our senior citizen tickets, we'd been invited to tap a small screen and to select—and thus reserve—our seats. The ticket seller, speaking slowly and distinctly, directed us to the doorway that would eventually lead to our theater. Blundering in the direction she'd pointed, we observed that adult beverages were now available from an impressive bar in the lobby. Mr. Doyle, however, did not care to have a martini with his popcorn.

We found our theater—Number 11—but the real shock came inside where fully reclining lounge seats had been installed for our viewing comfort. Or in my case, discomfort.

Monster things, they were. Wriggling myself back into my reserved seat, I felt like Lily Tomlin's Edith Ann. Or like Goldilocks in the largest Three Bears' chair. This seat was much too big for me. My legs didn't touch the floor and the concave back prevented me from sitting up straight. A fat headrest thrust my head uncomfortably forward. I was making small noises of dismay when Mr. Doyle demonstrated how a circular control, located on the seat arm, could tilt my chair back into a position similar to the one I'd assumed the week before during a dental cleaning. This seat was obviously designed for a much different American—a much fatter one. One who expected to watch a giant TV screen in the luxury of his/her home, ensconced in a Laz-E-Boy with snacks and remotes close at hand.

Struggling for comfort, I finally removed my shoes when the film started, and sat Indian-style in the immense seat so I could keep my back straight and my cervical vertebrae reasonably uncompromised. There was plenty of room for both shoes there in the seat with me.

The film was mildly entertaining, but I couldn't help contrasting the experience I was having to the events that shaped my early concept of "going to the movies."

The Center Mayfield was our local movie house, and in the nineteen forties, my father still called it "going to the pictures." The theater's marquee projected over the sidewalk and its dense constellation of light bulbs instantly warmed you as you stepped up to the ticket booth. With ticket in hand, you'd spent a few minutes enjoying the still shots from the current film and the gloriously illustrated movie posters luring you to coming attractions. Inside, the refreshment counter offered modest boxes of popcorn and movie candy—candy you couldn't find in drug stores. Mason Dots, Black Crows, Good 'n Plenty, Milk Duds that tasted slightly stale and Jujubees that tasted like perfume.

Movie-goers rarely worried about film start times. Folks wandered in whenever it was convenient, often right in the middle of a feature, and sat blissfully through the previews of coming attractions, newsreels, cartoons, short features, travelogues, the main feature, and often a double feature. When you sat through the whole offering and were beginning to view something you'd already seen, you'd poke a companion (or perhaps be the one to get poked) and whisper, "This is where we came in." And you'd rise and leave.

On Saturdays there were matinees with Superman and Batman and Tom Mix and extra cartoons, and Wednesday was the popular Dish Night. Dish Night made me nervous. On this night, the house lights were brought up, the curtains were drawn back—first the heavy drape, then the gauzy one, revealing the plain tan scrim. The Center Mayfield's manager came out and someone brought a big bowl of ticket stubs. As the manager drew out each winning number, a scream arose from different spots in the theater and a woman—the screamer—would run pell-mell down the aisle to claim her prize of dishes. Still screaming, she'd hug the manager, informing him at decibel level, "I never win anything!" Then the smiling manager would dive into the bowl for another ticket, and I would freeze with stage fright once again.

I was terrified my ticket number would be called. What would I do? Scream and run shrieking up the aisle, which seemed to be called for? I was sure I couldn't do that. If my ticket were called, could I just pretend it wasn't my number? But what if, while I was pretending, no one screamed and the ushers started looking around for the winner, checking people's tickets? I'd be found out and then look as foolish as if I'd screamed and run up to claim my prize. It was better to just avoid the Center Mayfield on Wednesday nights.

OLD DAME DANCING

The seats in the Center Mayfield were just ordinary seats. I think the upholstery was plush with the nap so worn your fingers could only recognize a remembrance of plush toward the edges. You didn't wrap your fingers over the edges of these seats lest you encounter ossified pieces of gum stuck there by your predecessors. There was nothing wrong with these seats though. No one expected anything better. There were fewer obese people then. Feet were expected to be placed decorously on the floor, not tilted up in the air. I never left the Center Mayfield with a crick in my neck.

∼

OLD DAME DANCING

THOSE WHO KNEW ME WHEN

*Understand that friends come and go,
but for the precious few you should hold on.*
Always Wear Sunscreen

I have a framed photograph of us around a table at Tavern-on-the-Green in Manhattan. Tavern-on-the-Green was a landmark, solid as New York itself. It's gone now, incredibly, but the nine of us are still here. We're older by two decades, but we're all still here. Amazing.

We went to high school together. Then came the college diaspora and after that ... well, the close ties slackened. We moved to different cities, then moved again to different ones in different states. There were cards at Christmas and a long season of birth announcements. We stayed in touch. Sort of. It's hard to stay in close touch when the reach extends from Fort Myers to New York to Detroit to Cincinnati to Cleveland and even to the small town in Massachusetts where I live. But twenty years ago, Karen, who has always kept us organized, hatched a plan to get together in Manhattan where Katie lives rather grandly in a large condo that looks down upon Gracie Mansion and the East River.

We were fifty-two years old then—thirty-four years past

OLD DAME DANCING

our high school graduation. But since then, we've gathered every other year—gathered in Katie's home for a three-day pajama party-henfest-museum-and-restaurant crawl, and I guess we're no longer middle-aged. (Sorry, ladies, but I've gotta call 'em as they are here.)

What do you say to someone you see so seldom? What do you say to women whose lives and CVs have diverged so widely? How do you ask the delicate questions about marriages and illnesses and children's heartbreaks? Isn't it all very awkward?

Awkward? God, no!

As landing gears touch the tarmac at LaGuardia and the red lights blink off, our cell phones start chiming.

"We're at Delta baggage."

"US Air Shuttle, I'm catching the bus over."

"Lyn's the last. She's coming in on JetBlue. Should be landing in seven minutes."

There are no awkward silences, no chances that we won't recognize each other. We still look exactly as we did in our senior pictures taken for the high school yearbook. Exactly! I swear it!

Talking nine to the dozen, we pick up a quick lunch in an airport snack bar. There is no funny business about separate checks. Paying for each other's lunches, dividing sandwiches, still talking, we pile into taxis for the trip to East End Ave. One year Lyn scored a limo.

And every year grows more precious.

Postscript: a year after this piece was written, an inevitable life change happened. Katie, our beautiful and gracious hostess passed away, leaving the rest of us shaken and sorrowing. The last line of this essay becomes especially poignant. Every year is more precious, but as we look back over the years we've shared, they are precious too.

ONE OFF THE BUCKET LIST

Well, my sister has a bucket list. I found out about it when I picked her up at the airport.

"But if you were going to travel all the way to Austria," I said, "how come you only stayed three days?"

"Because skiing in the Alps is on my bucket list," she told me, "and at age sixty-eight, I figured three days of Alpine skiing was all I could handle."

Oh.

A bucket list. A list of things you'd like to do before you kick the bucket.

I thought I ought to have one too. Trouble was, I wasn't sure what I'd list. Furthermore, I had no immediate plans to kick the bucket. But I thought a lot about it, and I looked for suggestions. It wasn't long before I saw one.

Driving toward Route 93, I saw a sandwich board advertising roller derby. Ha! Now I owned a bucket list. It had a single posting: attend a roller derby event.

That was six months ago. Then, last Saturday morning on the way to Route 93, there was the sandwich board again: "Roller Derby Tonight".

I resolved to go. I invited Mr. Doyle to join me.

"Girls in uniform?" he said. "You bet. I'm in!"

OLD DAME DANCING

So at a cost of sixteen dollars each—which I thought was steep; I mean, who actually *wants* to go to roller derby?—we bought our way into Shriner's Auditorium and instantly entered a new world. And I found out who actually wants to go to roller derby.

First, nice-looking people go to roller derby. Not all of them have purple mullets and painful-looking piercings. Moreover, the people we met spoke in complete, grammatically-correct sentences that did not depend on expletives to convey the message. They smiled; they were happy to be there, and the decibel level, though high, was not raucous. There was a cheerful, friendly atmosphere. As we left the lobby and stepped into the arena, we passed two of the teams in huddles under the bleachers, chanting and stamping their skates in anticipation.

"Sit anywhere," an attractive female attendant directed us cheerfully, "just don't step over the yellow line."

I obeyed instantly, not wishing to violate any rules in this new venue which might include being in the path of a roller derby skater.

We climbed into the bleachers and within minutes were told by the loudspeaker that we would be watching the Wicked Pissahs skate against the Cosmonaughties. And here they came! Two posses of them in uniforms blue and red with a variety of accessories that seemed to have no team designation: panties sequined or ruffled, patterned knee socks and other ornaments—which I learned later had all been purchased at Bruised Boutique, a New Hampshire sport shop dedicated to roller derby skaters.

Boston Derby Dames, the organization of which Wicked Pissahs and Cosmonaughties are affiliated, is itself a member of WFTDA—Women's Flat Track Derby Association.

The meet was a mystery to Mr. Doyle and me. We learned

that there were jammers and blockers, the former were skaters who tried to break through the pack while the latter tried to prevent them. Hipping seemed to be allowed although use of the hands was a violation. There were almost as many referees as skaters and one of these zebras was charged with following the progress of a jammer who broke out of the pack and skated a mad solo run around the track until she ran into traffic again. The ref skated with her, pointing a finger at the jammer while high in the air, her other hand signaled the points the skater was earning.

We made it to halftime, Mr. Doyle and I.

"Seen enough?" I asked.

"If you have," he said, "although I wouldn't mind looking over the tee-shirts in the lobby."

I could tell he was taken with the idea of owning a Wicked Pissahs shirt.

So we passed the lady selling cupcakes and surveyed the offerings of the Boston Derby Dames—Arkham Horrors, Boston Massacre, Nutcrackers. Mr. Doyle carefully studied the names and graphics before (wisely) deciding against the contemplated purchase, and we stepped out into the October evening. A light mist was falling. We walked happily toward the car. I was filled with satisfaction. One off my bucket list. I can't wait to tell my sister.

~

OLD DAME DANCING

I SLEPT THROUGH THAT ONE

I am at loss these days to join in conversations about popular—or even *arriviste*—film and TV stars, not to mention luminaries in the music field. I can leaf through *People* magazine without recognizing more than five names—and what's more, I don't care. Who *are* these people? And who cares about them? But it is politic to keep mum; I can only show my ignorance by asking questions, so I simply keep quiet and try look alert when people start discussing the rapper on the Super Bowl halftime show or who swept the Country Music Awards.

Trouble comes when a direct question is aimed at my head.

"Did you see such-and-such? (Plug in the name of a movie—any movie—right here.)

The truthful answer is: "I don't know."

That sounds dim, but what I do say doesn't sound much brighter.

"Did I see it?"

The question is addressed to my husband. We have a DVD player and a subscription to Netflix; each week a movie arrives and at some point in the week, we play it. Mr. Doyle watches it. I start to watch it too, but—I don't know—at some point I nod off and awaken near the end of the film. Very few films make much of an impression.

Our pubic library has an extensive film collection, and from time to time, one or the other of us will borrow a film.

"I hear this one is quite good," I say to Mr. Doyle, proud to have looked over the selection and made a choice.

"Yes," he says drily. "I thought was quite good last month when you slept through it."

OLD DAME DANCING

PARTY

And suddenly, mid-afternoon, cars turn the corner and pull to a stop. A party organizes in the backyard of the young couple who have just moved in across the street, and it all comes back—how it used to be when we were young.

We collected each other up into parties for the most nebulous reasons then; any excuse served. Maybe it was a holdover from the communal social habits of high school when we snatched at any chance to escape our parents' company. Maybe we were still conditioned to flash gatherings in dorm rooms. Or perhaps we were simply young enough and energetic enough to need and seek the constant reassurance of our peers around us. I don't know now. It's been years since that collective instinct to group rampaged.

But forty and fifty years ago—as young marrieds, new parents and parents-to-be—we were part of a circle of couples, interlocking puzzle pieces, essential to the whole. There were Saturday night bridge games, picnics, impromptu suppers of take-out pizza. And beyond this circle was a wider circle of friends who were included in the backyard barbeques organized to celebrate the birthdays of one friend or another who was reaching the ripe old age of thirty. Jokes about old age. Hysterically funny gifts. Hooting laughter and catcalls.

There were games of volleyball and bocce ball. Costume parties for Halloween and drunken gatherings on New Year's Eve where we began to notice that one or two of us imbibed too much too often and became sloppy or sometimes even vulgar.

Then slowly, the circles began to shrink. The Meyers moved away and so did the Scoutens, remembered only in the Christmas cards that continued to come—for a while. The Davenports got divorced. Two other couples simply stopped showing up.

When did it begin to be too much trouble to organize a gathering? How did we grow so old and stodgy? And I wonder, when did we become simply grateful, when there was a party, to be un-included?

Across the street, on this warm evening, the party is moving into its seventh hour. It's louder now. I hear the noise of slightly drunken voices raised. Our neighbors' house blazes in the night like the *Mary Celeste*.

My ghosts rise, playing Twister; Mary Danvenport in her stocking feet and wearing a tinsel crown, is thrown off balance by a clumsy lurch from Herbie Meyer who has a pirate's patch over one eye. There's a wheelbarrow full of beer bottles, and someone is cooling it with water from a garden hose.

The ghosts evaporate. The party across the street continues. I remember how it used to be. And I do not regret, on this warm night, that it is merely a memory.

∼

OLD DAME DANCING

Your age tells how long you've been on the road, not how far you've gotten.

SCOOP DISH

OLD DAME DANCING

SCOOP DISH

Scoop dish is one of our family's favorite meals. Basically, it's American chop suey with liberties taken. Ingredients are loosely organized around some sort of meat (either ground or leftover), macaroni, a chopped onion, a can of tomatoes perhaps and whatever cheese is handy. Once these ingredients are assembled, the contents of the refrigerator and pantry are inventoried and any likely contributors are voted into the dish. Spinach? Great. A handful of raisins? Why not. A dollop of salsa? Sure thing.

Here's the point: it is scoop dish as long as you can dig a serving spoon into the finished product and scoop out a generous serving of miscellany to whap onto your dinner plate.

Scoop dish is varied and interesting but you never quite know what you're going to get.

That's why this chapter is called Scoop Dish.

Dig in.

BREAKING A RECORD

Weather is not a competition
Ellen Wiklanski

We were having a mild winter. January was temperate, at least by January standards in New England, and we'd begun observing the lengthening days and telling each other that spring was right around the corner. Wouldn't be long now. The end was in sight. Then it happened. As a guy I know would say, in the midst of what happened just a few weeks later, "I don't know what gods we pissed off, but we're very very sorry."

Snow arrived with February. It came not in inches, but in feet. Then more came. And even more. Our personal snow piles—Mr. Doyle's and mine—rose above Doyle's head, and he is six feet tall. In my head, a familiar hymn played like a stuck recording:

In the bleak midwinter, icy wind made moan
Earth hard as iron, water like a stone
Snow had fallen, snow on snow on snow ...

That's what we had: snow on snow on snow. 98.6 inches had fallen in Boston by the end of the month. (More than that fell in the upper right-hand corner of Massachusetts where I live, but Boston takes little notice of what's going on to its immediate north.) The weather reporters on the TV news stations started to tell us enthusiastically that Boston could possibly log 100 inches this winter—a snow record. Records are important in Boston. Whether it's the Red Sox or the weather, whether it's the batting averages or the temperature, it doesn't matter—it just needs to be extreme. Great or terrible, the record is the thing. So it snowed like mad most of February, then the snow tapered off. The reporters' hysteria did not. Their daily reports grew frantic. What if the first day of spring arrived in March, and we hadn't busted through 100 inches? It seemed they were actually cheering for more of the damned stuff.

Whose side were they *on*?

Most of the citizenry, weary from shoveling and snow-blowing, from roof raking and from sopping up water that ice dams in gutters had sent cascading inside our houses—most of us didn't want to see another flake. We were wary of icy roads, of trains that wouldn't run, of the economy, which was turning to sludge and delivering body-blows to retailers and restaurateurs and people who depended on hourly paychecks. And I heard more than one mother swear that if her kids had one more snow day…well, she simply couldn't be held responsible for what might happen.

March arrived. The weather continued cold but with the time shift to daylight savings, at least there was—miraculously—sun.

On March 14, it rained. It rained the next day too. And then the rain shifted to snow. During the night I heard ice crunching as the occasional car drove down the street. I groaned and turned over. In the morning, all was white and news came that a new record had been set. Boston had blasted through the old one and had achieved more than 100 inches of snow this winter. 108.6 to be exact. (Even more in the northeast corner.)

OLD DAME DANCING

Most of the people I spoke to were sour about it. It was a record we had no interest in holding.

Years ago, for his column in *New Yorker*, E.B. White wrote an account of the hurricane that passed through New England in 1954. *("In The Eye of Edna")*. He had followed the nearly hysterical reporting of the hurricane's progress up from Rhode Island, and after one baffling update from a reporter in the field who "seemed to be in a sulk," White concludes: "It was one of those confused moments emotionally where the listener couldn't be quite sure what position the radio was taking—*for* hurricanes or *against* them."

That's been our position here as we've alternately fought the snow and listened to the weather pundits encourage the wretched weather to hit us again, all in pursuit of a record that doesn't mean a damned thing. Well, we've fought the fight and claimed the ultimate prize. The ultimate prize, if you ask me, is a booby.

Postscript. It's April and the snow is still three feet in parts of the yard, but the media is thinking spring, and has just given us the news that this year we could expect the worst allergy season on record. Let's hear it, Sufferers, one more for the record!

SOCIAL MEDIA FOR THE ANTI-SOCIAL

I don't understand Facebook. I really don't. That doesn't stop me, however, from having an FB account, and I tune into it faithfully everyday. Tune in—that's a term from the golden age of radio, isn't it? A time when they said things like tune in tomorrow for the next episode of the Lone Ranger/Little Orphan Annie/Inner Sanctum/whatever.

But I digress.

I tune into Facebook every morning after I've checked my email and glanced at the headlines in *The Boston Globe*. Then I bring up what I now understand is my Timeline—and by the way, whatever happened to my Wall? People were always writing on my Wall. "I've written on your Wall," they'd say, and I'd think, "How rude." I used to be punished for writing on walls. Now they've stopped writing on my Wall.

Where was I?

Oh. Tuning into Facebook.

Okay. So I bring up Facebook to snoop around and find out what folks I know are up to, and you would be amazed at what they are up to! They are dining in restaurants and showing photos of what they are eating and drinking to prove they are actually where they say they are. They are sending maps so I can pinpoint their locations. I can't think how many glasses of red wine I've seen with some restaurant, all dark and romantic and slightly out of focus in the background behind the red wine. They are in airports waiting for flights to New Zealand and Venice. They are on mountaintops gazing at views blue and distant or admiring the autumn colors in Vermont. Even if I posted on Facebook, which as I've explained I do not, my posts wouldn't be in the same league as my friends. What would I do? Post a shot of the waiting room in the veterinarian's office? The Redstone Shopping Center in Stoneham, Massachusetts? "Here I am outside Dress Barn?"

I have a photo on my Facebook page. It's the same photo that was put there when someone set up the page for me. It is just my back and I am wearing a hat because I didn't really want to be recognized, and you might not know it is me except I am holding a sword and I am probably one of the few persons anyone knows who regularly practices with a sword. But among Facebook followers, photos are important and people are always updating them. "So and so has changed his profile picture." And sure enough, there's another close-up. Or feet! I've seen feet on Facebook! I regularly see the results of pedicures, and a guy I know took a picture of *his* feet in a hot tub. He had not, it was clear, had a pedicure. He didn't care. He's the same guy who had himself photographed in his new shower—just from the chest north, of course.

But as I scroll through my Timeline in the morning, people are showing up who I don't even know. Down and down I swipe, and people I've never met come flashing past me, and while most of them look like very nice people, there are always one or two that make me think, "Good Heavens!"

And then I think, "How did they get there, these people?" and "Who *are* they?"

Once in a while I dare to write a comment on the Timelines of very close friends, but I don't go so far as to "Like" someone's post. Apparently when you like a post, the news radiates out to everyone you ever knew. I am really starting to wonder about of some of my friends who are quite pleasant in person but whose political or artistic tastes, I'm finding out through Facebook, are quite offensive. I keep my own political persuasions quite close to my chest.

Now social media isn't limited to Facebook, of course, and you might be surprised to learn I also have Twitter and Linked-In accounts. These affiliations were not my idea. Dickie felt they were advantageous business connections, and he set up the accounts and then explained, more or less, how to use them before he rushed off.

I want you to know I have never tweeted or twitted, and I don't know when to use a hash tag or even what a hash tag means. So I ignore Twitter.

Linked-In now, Linked-In is another matter. I guess people I know—and some of them I don't know well—troll through Linked-In, discover I'm there too and seek me out. They send me invitations to link. These invitations unsettle me, although they do make me feel popular. I have only a vague idea what linking entails, but it seems rude to rebuff these advance, so I agree to link. Then, the next thing I know one of these linked buddies is endorsing me. I can't imagine why. I am retired, and here they are, endorsing my skills. Someone explained to me that I am supposed to endorse them right back. Maybe these linkees earn some kind of extra credit for the number of endorsements. I don't know. The other day I was congratulated on my Linked-In anniversary. I didn't even know we were a couple.

Social media is everywhere. Waze, my current GPS of choice, doesn't just direct you to your destination, it depends on FB-connected subscribers to inform each other of potholes, hidden police presence and traffic jams. Waze is always interested in knowing if I want to connect with the other Facebookers who are on the road with me. Well, of course I don't!

Texting and Instagram not only put people in instant (and constant) touch, but have created a new genre of communication that corrupts the English language into misspellings and reliance on emojis. Emoji. I didn't know what those are. Had to look it up on Google to learn they were small digital images or icons that express ideas and emotions. Did you know that? Ah, I thought, so that's what all those smiley and sad faces are—emojis. I mean, where have I been? Why am I always the last to know?

I suppose social media has surged ahead, and as soon as someone like me learns what an emoji is, an emoji is passé. I'm already hopelessly dated. An anti-socialist in the social media world.

CHARLIE CARD BLISS

> *He may ride forever 'neath the streets of Boston*
> *He's the man who never returned*
> Bess Hawes and Jacqueline Steiner

"We could go in on the Orange Line."

It was the eve of the July Fourth holiday, Dickie had an appointment with a client in Boston, I was going along under my old creative director's hat, and neither of us wanted to cope with the city's holiday exodus. Still, Dickie looked doubtful.

"Do you know how?" he asked me.

"The only tricky part is finding a parking space at Oak Grove. Provided we can do that, the rest is simple."

The single benefit of the pre-holiday hysteria was that a few souls were escaping Boston even earlier than usual, and there actually was a space in the Oak Grove parking lot.

"What do we do now?" Dickie demanded.

"Now? Now I will introduce you to the miracle of the Charlie card."

We made our way up the stairs, into the Oak Grove terminal and directly up to my friend the MBTA customer service rep. I pointed back at Dickie.

"This man needs a Charlie card."

OLD DAME DANCING

All customer service reps should be as good-humored and patient as the Pleasant Man of Oak Grove. Day after day he painstakingly teaches otherwise intelligent and productive human beings to use the simple, intuitive mechanics of the Charlie card vending machine. Dickie has a degree in electrical engineering from a very prestigious college and an advanced degree from a famous Boston institution of higher learning, but I noticed that he stumbled through the process, leaning heavily on the prompts of the jolly customer service rep.

Later, as we stood on the platform waiting for the train, Dickie held his new Charlie card in both hands and gazed at it with pride.

"Now I have a Charlie card," he marveled.

"You're a citizen," I told him.

The train arrived and we glided aboard. Dickie was humming *Charlie on the MTA*.

"Do you remember Scollay Square?" he asked abruptly.

"Where Charlie's wife handed him a sandwich?"

"I was dating a nurse from Beth Israel Hospital," he reminisced, "and I got lost in Scollay Square on my way to pick her up."

If you know approximately when they tore down Scollay Square, you'll get the clue that Dickie wasn't born yesterday. But here's the thing about Dickie—even at his age he has an engaging enthusiasm and an engineer's fascination with new things that is childlike and therefore charming. He continued to marvel about his Charlie card all the way to State Street.

"I could do this any time," he told me happily. "Just go to Oak Grove ..."

"... provided there's a parking space," I amended.

"Yes, I'll just find a parking space, and I'll take my Charlie card ..." A new thought struck him. "I'll get one for Jean! Yes! We'll both go into Boston for the day and walk around. Have lunch. What is it—a dollar-seventy one way? Wow. For less than seven bucks we can have a day in Boston. Wow!"

I am reminded that Joseph Campbell counseled folks to follow their bliss, and as the train from Oak Grove bucketed along toward State Street and our appointment in the financial district, I considered how Dickie was unconsciously heeding Campbell's advice. Here, with a brand new Charlie card in his wallet, he was following his bliss along the MBTA's Orange Line.

OLD DAME KVETCHING

Look, what's the point of elbowing into your eighth decade if you aren't allowed to bitch a little? So I'm giving myself permission to *kvetch*. Fine word, *kvetch*. I learned it from Dickie along with *blech*. *Blech* is something like *kvetch*, except it's a nuance away. *Kvetching* is bitching and *bleching* is...well, it's like whining. So this is what I want to *kvetch* about.

Software upgrades:

I resist most of them on the grounds that while they give you something new, they usually take something else away—some convenience I've come to depend on. But even I have to cave to the inevitable, and I caved last Thursday. First I had to convince Mr. Doyle to handle the upload (download?) while I fled to another part of the house and put my fingers in my ears. I could still hear him though.

"Damn it!"

Then, "Why won't they recognize your password?" he asked the ether. I knew he wasn't talking to me exactly, but I murmured the answer: Because my passwords are never accepted by any site. Ever!

He prevailed however, and on the sixth try, Apple relented and acknowledged my password, and thus armed with IOS 8, I joined the rest of civilization.

Now I have graphics that are far more difficult to read but to mitigate this, all the programs load much more slowly and the ipad hangs up constantly.

Packaging:

Now here's good reason to *kvetch*! I'm tired of buying stuff in child-proof containers. I've had the same aspirin bottle for years, and it has a good, old-fashioned screw top. When the tablets in it are gone, I buy a new bottle and struggle to get the damn thing open. When I finally succeed, I decant the new aspirin into the old bottle. Then I don't screw the lid down tight. When I have a headache, I don't want to have to break into a vault to get relief. I realize that a C-H-I-L-D could open this bottle and eat all my aspirin, but since there are no children in this house and none come to visit, I do not feel honor-bound to child-proof my aspirin.

Products encased in hard plastic shells:

They may be tamper-proof but they're also consumer-proof. I've stabbed these shells with kitchen knives, tried inserting knives between the plastic and the cardboard, even attacked from the back, and all with little result. And if I do manage to pierce the shell, savage plastic shards are ready to create a paper cut on steroids.

Robocalls:

Listen, I know who you are. We have caller I.D. We don't pick up when you call. However, we do stand up and cross the room, Mr. Doyle or I, to squint at caller I.D. The squinter then calls out, "Do you know anyone in Springfield, Illinois? In Waco, Texas? Do you know anyone in area code 202? No? Then I won't answer." The do-not-call list does not work.

People who allow their three-year-olds to record answering machine messages:

I know your kid is cute. I know the little character is begging to record. But your greeting is unintelligible and I usually hang up in confusion and disgust. When your phone doesn't ring, it'll be me.

I have a friend—a lad in his mere 50s—who claims he is a curmudgeon-in-training. Now when it comes to *kvetching*, he is just getting started.

∼

ENDING THE CHRISTMAS POTLATCH

Christmas will soon be at our throats again, and so I am forced, once again, to contemplate the Christmas potlatch. Now I am not speaking of the gifts you give your near and dear—your children and spouses and so forth. I am thinking of those outside the family circle; good friends, certainly, but folks with whom you have developed, over the years, extensive, even elaborate, gift exchanges that are out of proportion to your mutual relationship and that have become like run-away carriages.

These ceremonies start innocently enough. Maybe you receive a plate of decorated cookies from the neighbors next door. You are touched and pleased and naturally you feel you need to respond in kind. Decorated cookies just aren't your thing however, and anyway, *they* had given cookies so you had to think of something entirely other. So you rack your brain until you remember that little jar candle with the spruce scent. So you tie a pretty ribbon on it and leave it in a gift bag on their doorstep.

Well, it turns out that Gloria just *adores* spruce and she determines that *you* must be fond of scented candles, so next year, she leaves a gift bag on your doorstep that contains a full-sized jar candle—one of those big jars from a candle manufacturer known for its luxury (i.e. expensive) candles. And, just for good measure, she throws in another plate of those decorated cookies. Now you are back in the same predicament as the year before—trying to think up a creative response to this double gift, but you can't retaliate with a dinky little spruce jar candle. You have to think of something else and end up spending more than you should.

And so it goes on like that, year after year. The original plate of decorated cookies has morphed into gift bags filled with wrapped goodies for every family member, including the pets, and every year you are racking your brain and pillaging your checking account in order to hold up your end and participate appropriately in this particular Christmas potlatch, which may just be one of several potlatches you've innocently strayed into.

What to do about this?

Probably the best approach is the straight-forward one. Select a day in, say July, and speak to Gloria in the backyard.

"You know, I was thinking about Christmas," you could say, wiping the beads of sweat off your upper lip.

This might surprise Gloria, since she's been thinking along the lines of putting some manure on her rose bushes, and Christmas has not entered her mind.

But you press bravely on.

"I was thinking that maybe this coming Christmas we could do something different about gifts. Maybe we could take the money we'd spend on gifts for each other's families and donate it to a charity."

Chances are excellent that Gloria will be delighted and as eager you are to end the Christmas potlatch. And if she is disappointed...well...just consider that disappointment breeds character and stick to your guns.

Here's one cautionary note: you may find a plate of

decorated cookies on your doorstep again this Christmas. Gloria may just not be able to resist. But if you do find those cookies, bring them inside. Eat them. Tell Gloria that you enjoyed them, but don't, under any circumstances, retaliate. To do so will plunge you right back into the Christmas potlatch.

∽

OLD DAME DANCING

THE ANGEL WHO STOPS FOR A BEER

"The angel who is bringing me money stops for a beer."

Thus does Mr. Doyle begin the story of his personal financial equilibrium.

"Seinfeld," he explains, "has a belief that in the end, you come out even. For instance, if he were to lose twenty bucks on the subway on his way to work, somehow, by the end of the day, somebody will come to him and say: 'Seinfeld, I've got twenty dollars worth of comp tickets to the game. Take them!"

"I thought about that," Doyle says, "and I realized I've always had a similar superstition about my life, and it goes like this:

On his way out of Heaven, the angel who is bringing me money stops in some celestial bar for a beer. And he says to the bartender, 'I can't stay long because Doyle's got money coming to him and I gotta go down and take him the money.'

Now somewhere down the bar somebody pipes up.

'Doyle? *That* bum! He owes *me* money, and I just finished my beer.'

So *that* angel comes down from Heaven too and now it's a race. Often I won't know which angel arrives on earth first—the one who is bringing me the bill or the one who is bringing me the money to *pay* the bill. Sometimes they arrive practically together; sometimes one is pathetically late. But I've noticed that their arrivals are twin events, and if just one angel shows up, I can be certain that the other will be along shortly. It's gotta be celestial. I *must* be angels. And I believe in it!"

THE MOTEL CLERK

That June when my son came to work as a summer intern in the advertising agency where I was a principal, he also accepted a job—a *paying* job—as a night clerk in a local motel. When he left the agency in the late afternoon, he checked in (in a manner of speaking) to the motel. I'm sure the job had hours of boredom, punctuated with occasional bursts of drama, some of which involved the police or the rescue squad. But once he told a tale of an encounter at the motel desk, and his story flooded my maternal heart with gratitude.

This, then, is the way Jamie told it:

So these two guys come into the motel—salesmen. They give me their names and check in, and I hand them their keys. Then one guy asks if there are any messages for him.

"Yes," I tell him. "There is one."

And I hand him the message. He reads it. The other guy watches him read it.

"Who's it from?" the second guy wants to know.

"Ted. It's from Ted."

"Ted? What's he want?"

"Aw," says the first guy. "Nothing really. He's just scared. He just needs someone to tell him he's okay and he is loved."

I laughed. "You sound just like my mother," I told him.

Ah, the lad had been paying attention all along.

OLD DAME DANCING

THE ODESSY OF THE PURPLE HAT

> *When I'm an old lady, I shall wear purple*
> *With a red hat that doesn't go.*
> *Jenny Joseph*

Her sixtieth birthday was approaching and she was feeling lousy about it. It was mud season in Maine, a fierce head cold had settled in her sinuses and none of her three children, living as they were in three other states, had said anything about her birthday. But who wanted to turn sixty anyway? She'd been asking this often.

A bell tinged in the house, signaling someone had turned into the driveway, and sure enough, a UPS truck came bumping up the grade, sloshing through puddles, the wipers beating furiously. The deliveryman swung up to the house with his parcel, and dived back to the warmth of the dry truck.

Mystified, she noted the package had come from a friend out-of-state. She pried it open, and there it was—a purple satin hat. The hat was a shiny pillbox considerably enhanced with a huge, swatch of purple netting tied off to one side in a bow. It had a veil. Also purple.

She tried it on in front of a mirror and for the first time in eight days, laughed. Laughed right out loud.

"That hat immediately changed things," she said.

Her husband came home and told her to dress for dinner. He was taking her out. And as he steered her into the restaurant, she saw all three sons and their wives and her grandchildren waiting for her at the table.

"Surprise!" they caroled.

And later, as they all posed for family photos, she insisted on wearing the purple satin hat.

"I have just the thing for you," she said when her friend Nancy needed something appropriate to wear to a costume parade at her husband's college reunion. Now Williams's colors are purple and white and nothing in that parade could compete with the outrageous purple satin hat. Nancy walked off with the prize.

At a restaurant table overlooking the Piscataqua River, which divides New Hampshire from Maine, the purple satin hat came back to me. It was my birthday—the one ushering me into my eighth decade—and I suppose it served me right. There it was, nestled in green tissue, the purple hat, it's outrageousness undiminished. I promised my companions that I would wear the hat. I would guard it well and send it forth into situations where its purpleness would do useful work. So just now it is going to a talent show, and it is going on the head of yet another Nancy who will wear it with an outrageous sense of style and *joie de vivre*. And once more, the purple hat will make people smile.

THINGS I WILL NEVER KNOW

These are some of the things I will never understand:

Fibonacci numbers sequence: 1 / 1 / 2 / 3 / 5 / 8 / 13 / 21 / 34 / 55 / 89 / 144. Well, I didn't understand Fibonacci numbers when I wrote this, but now I do—sort of. It is said you can see Fibonacci numbers in the globe of an artichoke or the scales of a pinecone. Supposedly the sequence can explain how rabbits reproduce. That's the part I don't understand.

Why any wine should cost more than thirty dollars. Hell, I don't understand why any wine should cost more than ten dollars.

How to record *anything* on a VCR.

Why Paris Hilton was famous in the first place, and where did she go? And has her disappearance set a precedent—as many hope it has—for the Kardashians?

Why, when I have to swerve to pass a bicyclist on my right, there is *unfailingly* an oncoming car to my left?

How DOS (Disc Operating System) worked. Only I don't have to understand this anymore because somebody made DOS obsolete. But while it was still around, and while Dickie was trying to teach it to me, it made my life miserable.

Why anyone would care if the label on what my grandmother used to call a pockabook says *Coach*.

OLD DAME DANCING

    Phi: the golden ratio the golden ratio—1.628033989—which was used to build the Parthenon and also appears in the musical compositions of Bartok and Debussy. (I didn't make that up. I copied it from somewhere.)
    Ditto pi.
    Why electricity doesn't leak out of the wall sockets and zap us.
    Why small children instantly recover from any illness or weird rash upon entering a pediatrician's office.

∼

THINGS I THINK I DO KNOW

These are some of the things I think I understand.

The Rule of Thirds.

The rhyme schemes of Shakespearean, Petrachran and Spenserian sonnets

Shakespearean: abab/cdcd/efef/gg

Petrarchan (or Italian): abab/cdcd/efef/gg

Spenserian: abab/bcbc/cdcd/ee

The role of gluten in rising bread.

How to operate a standard shift car without giving passengers whiplash.

Why Robert B. Parker was a brilliant writer, although I am growing less sure about John Updike.

That cinnamon repels ants.

That you can get a knife through the tough hide of a butternut squash quite easily if you first treat the squash to a brief whirl in the microwave.

Work-and-turn versus work-and-tumble. (Terms used in the printing industry)

That Magic Eraser will remove mildew from fiber cement siding.

~

OLD DAME DANCING

THIS IS SOMEONE'S LUNCH

One summer my daughter declared she was sick of thinking and she would, on her summer break from college, seek a job where she could mindlessly accomplish a task. In a short time she found such a job—a job making sandwiches for a canteen. You know those small trucks that look they're made out of aluminum foil? The ones that come careening into the parking lots in industrial parks, hooting their distinctive horns as a signal for workers to come out and purchase food for lunches and coffee breaks? One of those outfits would supply her summer job.

So every morning Elizabeth rose well before dawn and went to work building sandwiches that she would wrap and watch loaded into a tinfoil truck. She is an intense person, Elizabeth, and she became very focused on this work.

"I try to remember," she said, "that this sandwich I am making is someone's lunch. Maybe this sandwich is the single thing that this worker has to look forward to in his day. Maybe it's the best break in a job that is tedious or uncomfortable. And so I remember this every time I make a sandwich, and I make sure that the food in it is neat—not with lettuce hanging out sloppily, and not with the tuna just glopped in the middle instead of spread to the edges and not with the bread slices not matched up squarely."

There was no note of altruistic satisfaction in her tone. No whiff of nobility or high-mindedness. She made this statement rather grimly, I thought, and I knew she could see the worker who would eat this sandwich. She had probably envisioned an entire life story for him. He would have a mother with a cancer diagnosis, or have a car payment due that would leave him strapped—if he could scrape up the money at all, that is. Or he'd have a boss who was unreasonable or cranky, or he'd be facing an evening of ineffable dullness with nothing more hopeful that a dreary TV schedule, a boiled hot dog and a beer.

Elizabeth built sandwiches all that summer, but thinking about what she was doing never escaped her. She never forgot that she was making someone's lunch.

∽

OLD DAME DANCING

THE SEX LIFE OF HANGERS

This is about wire coat hangers. I despise them. All of them. But I especially despise the thin white ones that dry cleaners give you. (Well, I suppose they don't *give* them to you; they probably build the cost into the price of dry cleaning, which has certainly gotten very high, in case you haven't noticed.) Anyhow, they sneak into the house, those hangers, and infest the closets, and once they're in there, they breed. They breed in the dark privacy at the closets' backs, and they are insidious, sexually rapacious pests. I am forced to go into Mr. Doyle's closet every so often to exterminate them. I am neither gracious nor graceful when I do this. I am loud and bitchy.

"How do these things get *in* here?" I yell.

"Why do you let them in?" I continue at high volume. "You *know* how I feel about wire hangers."

"What has a wire hanger ever done to you?" Doyle asks innocently.

"Done? Well, I'll tell you what they've done. They just slump when you hang something on them. They fold at the back and—sloop—there's your jacket on the closet floor."

No, they don't stand up to the job at all, wire hangers. And Doyle! Doyle is everlastingly hanging sport coats or heavy sweaters on them, and they just drop their shoulders and give up the ghost. They droop and half the garment slides off and dangles and the closet is just a mess.

And for another thing, they get all tangled up with each other once they overtake a closet. I suspect that's how they breed. In fact, I'm sure of it. And I am forced to stand there, uncoupling and pulling apart and grumbling.

There is only one good thing to say about wire coat hangers: they are useful for breaking into locked cars. My late mother, the irrepressible Maggie, locked her keys in her car with such regularity that she always kept a coat hanger in her car as insurance against emergency lock-outs. Of course we pointed out that the hanger was locked in with the keys, but its very presence reassured Maggie, and she stood ready to rush to the aid of other hapless victims of car lock-outs.

Car break-ins notwithstanding, I have no good words to say about wire coat hangers. All that coupling and multiplying and carrying on in the closet. Let two wire coat hangers get together in a closet and next thing you know they've reproduced and hatched a whole litter.

I'll tell you what there is around the house that *doesn't* have a sex life. Socks. In the beginning you have a pair. They say it takes two—well, not in this case. First you have a pair, and then you don't. They're asexual, socks. They simply don't breed. One of them either dies or is abducted. I wouldn't mind so much if they both went, but no. And there we are, left wondering what to do with a widowed sock. I usually slip it on my hand and dust.

∼

YOU CAN'T MISS IT

"Just go straight until you come to the second stop sign, then it's a left and another left, turn right and there you are. You can't miss it."

Oh, yes I can! And I've proved dozens of times that I can. That phrase assuring me that I'll easily find it dooms the whole thing.

Moreover, that damning statement has corollaries. Like this one: "There's nothing to it."

"Sure," I told the minister, "I'll do a bread baking project with the church school kids; the only thing is, I don't know how to work that monster of a stove in the church kitchen."

"Oh, there's nothing to it," he assured me, happy to have recruited a patsy for the bread baking chore. Then he hurried off to take an urgent call. I couldn't see his face but I suspect he was grinning. Turns out he didn't know how the thing worked either.

Unconvinced that there was nothing to it, I applied to the chairman of the house committee, who admitted he didn't know how to operate the thing. The custodian didn't have a clue. Finally the Youth Group leader persuaded her husband, a professional chef, to come along and light the oven for me, and as he struggled, I observed that there really was something to it.

Here's another: "You'll never notice a thing."

As soon as I hear this, I flash on computers. Computers are always needing upgrades or downloads; new software has been developed—software with sleek lines and upswept fins. This software, of course, is very easy to install. Why, there's nothing to it. And it will meld so smoothly with the clunky old programs I have been happily running that I will never notice a thing.

Ha. I repeat, *Ha!*

But over my protestations and compelling arguments against the installation, my business partner elbows me aside and completes the installation. And guess what? I notice. I notice that something didn't install correctly or has booby-trapped an existing fond feature or has scrambled the fritzwhang and I can no longer print copy.

"I'm noticing!" I holler from my desk. "I notice a thing!"

His head appears around the corner of my office and he is actually surprised. "No kidding?" he says, obviously believing it's my fault. "Here, lemme see."

And back under the hood he goes, mumbling and muttering while I impatiently wait out this latest attempt to make things easier.

And that's another phrase I mistrust—easy. "It's really very easy." It's really very easy to assemble … to read … to open … to install the upgrade.

Grasp the tab and pull. Yeah? Me and who else? The childproof aspirin bottle, the clever pop-top dog food can, the chips packaged in a product resembling microfilm, the Swiss cheese in a plastic envelope with a zipper that is supposed to miraculously reseal itself to maintain freshness. None of it works as promised.

Is it really very easy? Or is it just me?

OLD DAME DANCING

THOSE WHO RESCUE OUR HEARTS

There are two stories here, both rather sad, unless—like me—you choose to view them as redemptive.

Bud arrived just when he said he would—a few minutes early in fact. He backed the truck slowly up the service drive toward the barn. Ann Marie had finished her business, and she and her vet tech were packing their van. She acknowledged Bud with a small salute.

We watched his arrival from the kitchen window.

"Please," my daughter said, "could you take my checkbook and pay him? The check's all filled out except for the dollars. I wasn't sure of the final amount. And could you also ask Bud to please...take off...the halter?"

Since my self-designed job description was to provide emotional support, I overrode my resistance to go out there. I took the checkbook and went to meet the truck, stepping respectfully around the now-still horse. The two heavyset men in the cab looked like clones of each other; the one I took to be Bud began backing the truck carefully over the lawn. The passenger gazed at me dolefully. I went around to the driver's door.

"I'm her mom. She asked me to give you the check."

"Ma'am."

"She wasn't sure of the total."

He told me.

Filling in the amount, I saw my hand was shaking.

When I handed over the check, Bud presented a small card with words about the Rainbow Bridge.

"And she wondered if you would remove his halter?"

"Aw, sure...sure I will."

"I already put the halter in the barn," Ann Marie said as she came up to us.

She and I exchanged a few words, but I was in a hurry to get back to the house before Bud began doing what he had to do.

Liz, her eyes swollen, had two cups of hot tea ready in the kitchen. When I took my tea bag to the sink, Bud's truck was already heading up the road.

"Where does he take them?"

"Somewhere up in Maine. His son is always with him and usually his wife rides along. I don't know what we'll do when Bud goes."

The "we" was the local horse community—a surprisingly large and close-knit freemasonry that depends on Bud—and on each other—to fill some hard, life-and-death needs that arise in the normal course of things.

"He's careful. He never cuts off their tails."

I stood at the sink and reflected on the gentle humanity of people like Bud who not only take on the awkward task of horse disposal, but who do it gently and with respect for the animal and the owner. The Rainbow Bridge card was on the kitchen table. I knew Liz would keep it.

The woman thought she heard crying in the adjoining cubicle. When the crying accelerated into sobbing, she quietly stepped next door. Her office mate's head was on the desk; he was drenched in grief. Slowly at first, then in a flood, his story poured out.

He was ill. Medical costs, not covered by insurance, had eroded his savings. Circumstances were forcing him to move to a place where pets were explicitly forbidden, and that very morning, he had taken his beloved Italian greyhound to an animal shelter. He'd left it there, believing that the little dog would be euthanized. The man's soul was in anguish.

"Why didn't you call a rescue group?" his co-worker wanted to know. Involved, as she was in Border collie rescue, it seemed to her incomprehensible that someone wouldn't take the breed rescue course of action. He was astounded. He had never heard of such organizations.

"If I'd done that, he might not be put to sleep?"

"Well, look," she said briskly. "Let's find an Italian greyhound rescue rep and see if anything can be done."

A quick web search, a couple of phone calls, and soon Mary of IG Rescue was making plans to meet the fellow at the shelter where he had turned in his beloved pet. As well, Mary made a pre-visit call to the shelter to introduce herself and to claim a registered rescue group's "first dibs" accommodation. Yes, they would hold the dog until Mary and the former owner could get there.

"I've never been hugged so much in my life," Mary claimed later. "But I was able to assure him that his dog would have a good, loving home, and that he could contact the new owners so he could be satisfied that his friend was in a good circumstance. Oh, and this dog's a sweetie. He'll be so loved!"

It is terribly difficult to let a beloved animal go. But when parting times come to an animal owner, it is of untold comfort to walk with folks who are able to give us and our animals what each needs. The rescue reps, the sympathetic veterinarians, the friends who understand, and even the guys

OLD DAME DANCING

who slowly back up their trucks and respectfully carry off the horses that are loved still and always—these are the ones who rescue our hearts. These are the ones who help us heal.

Please, dear God...Bless the beasts and singing birds and guard with tenderness all things that have no words.

Kate Braestrup, Blessing for a Moose

OLD DAME DANCING

THERE'S A DANCE IN THE OLD DAME YET

Once I saw my mother-in-law—the grandmother of seven and carrying some thirty extra pounds—dance the Texas Bop. She was light on her feet, even with those extra pounds, and she could still roll each foot forward and over in that weird, rhythmic maneuver that is the hallmark of the Texas Bop. And I remember seeing my own grandmother at age 89, daintily hike up the hem of her dress and execute a few Highland Fling steps—the kick, point and waggle. "The heelin' and toein'" she called it. Old dames both of them, and still dancing.

My dance was the Jitterbug. I came to adolescence in the 'fifties—and in Cleveland—the city where disc jockey Alan Freed coined the term rock 'n roll. The place where Bill Randle (Station WERE) introduced Elvis Presley, Bobby Darin and Fats Domino. Like its cousins the Lindy, the Bop, and the White River Junction Stomp, the Jitterbug bounced out of Swing. (Double-step on left, sink on the right back-step, left, repeat). Easy and relaxed or exuberant and acrobatic featuring athletic lifts and swings, the Jitterbug was danced in ballrooms and gymnasiums. And it was my dance. Mine. Oh, I've waltzed and foxtrotted. I've Frugged and Ponied. I've Twisted and Strolled, but my dance is the Jitterbug.

I don't do much Jitterbugging these days. Partners from high school who might still remember the steps, are thin on the ground, for one thing. And for another, my present husband's many good features include two left feet. Still, when I catch a few strains of just the right music, the old steps begin. It can be a golden oldie Swing tune like *In The Mood* or *One o' Clock Jump*. It can be the smooth, casual Del Vikings sound of *Come Go With Me*. Or, if no one's around, it'll be Billy Joel, wild and raw, with *Only The Good Die Young*.

Old? Sure. But still dancing. Whenever the music is right; whenever I get the chance.

How about you? Are you doing any dancing these days? I'll bet you are—or you should be—if only in your mind.

So here I am, deep in my eighth decade and still dancing —a twenty-first century incarnation of Don Marquis's alley cat Mehitabel, who claims she has a human soul. "oh the queens i have been and the swell feeds i have ate", she reminisces, and closing her eyes, she concludes:

> *my youth i shall never forget*
> *but there s nothing i really regret*
> *wotthehell wotthehell*
> *there s a dance in the old dame yet*
>   Don Marquis: Archy and Mehitable

∼

OLD DAME DANCING